step away from the crayons

BUILDING A STRONG B2B BRAND

ALAN BRIGHT   **PHIL PARR**

Matador
BUSINESS

ISBN: 978-1848760-226

Published by
Troubador Publishing Ltd
9 De Montfort Mews, Leicester, LE1 7FW, UK
Tel: +44 (0) 116 255 9311   Fax: +44 (0) 116 255 9323
Email: enquiries@troubador.co.uk

Printed in the UK by
TJ International Ltd,
Padstow, Cornwall

Matador Business is an imprint of Troubador Publishing Ltd.

Contents

Acknowledgements

The main body text face used in this book is
Linotype 'Brighton', designed by Alan Bright in 1979.
We particularly thank Linotype (www.linotype.com)
for their assistance and interest in this project.

A special thank you to Nigel Temple for saying
'I think you need to write a book guys…'

We would also like to thank others involved in making
this book happen, specifically to Pat Bates, Sue Drummond,
Ruth Parr, Sally Bright, Jacqui Murnin and Rupert Chislett
for their invaluable insights and grammatical expertise.

Artwork produced by Twentyfive Creative LLP.

Design and typography
Richard Edgerton and Jason Ward

Contact us
If you would like an in-depth brand diagnostic undertaken
for you, or assistance to build your brand strategy,
Alan and Phil can be contacted via **www.twentyfive.co.uk**

Introduction

We'd like to start with some good news! Firstly, brand is very probably not what you think it is, and you are not in the minority. The concept of brand is widely misunderstood. Secondly, building a strong brand does not have to be financially prohibitive for even the smallest companies, because it isn't rocket science! Virtually no company, particularly in the Business-to-Business (B2B) sector, gets it right, so again, you're not alone. Most importantly, you can make a start right now, as long as you set your sights on the long haul. Creating, developing and maintaining a healthy brand is not a quick fix — but it is well worth the effort as we will demonstrate.

brand
is very probably not what you think it is

Let's give you a quick overview of how we came to understand the world of 'holistic' branding. It's been quite a journey — exhilarating, frustrating, challenging and often just plain hard work over the years. Interestingly we came to understand brand from completely different backgrounds and different time spans. Phil comes from the hard-headed, precise world of IT and Project Management and worked predominantly within large financial institutions, whereas Alan comes from a design background working for a variety of companies from multinationals to small to medium enterprises (SMEs).

Back in the late sixties guys like Wally Olins, Michael Wolff, Michael Peters, and Peter Hatch (whom Alan worked for), were already leading the way in the London design scene with the concept that everything a company produced visually should have a constant 'family' feel.

Starting with the company logo, these design companies developed intricate corporate identity manuals which dictated everything that a company produced visually. These mammoth and costly efforts were often contained in thick ring binders – immaculately designed and produced of course – and ran to many, many pages. The manuals had tear-off swatches of the primary, secondary and tertiary colours that could be used by printers to ensure accurate colour matching. They specified which typefaces were to be used, and the relationship of font sizes and weights, and covered stationery templates, advertising templates, brochure templates, and every other kind of template you can think of! They addressed external signage, company dress codes, vehicle liveries – always with precise instructions of where the logo could be used, what size, how much space had to be left around the logo and so on – and it worked. Corporate clients developed a clearly identifiable style that customers could easily recognise and, with recognition, trust was built. The clamour for 'corporate identity' raged like wildfire and advertising to consumers (B2C) by companies such as Bang & Olufsen became almost iconic. The B2B sector followed suit with corporate brochures and other special items such as the famous Pirelli calendar – beautiful girls captured by world-famous photographers. (Designers became really obsessed in trying to get their hands on one of those limited editions!)

Since those heady days, many companies have become increasingly aware that there is actually much more to brand than just the visual look. Somehow, somewhere the word 'brand' was adopted into the commercial dictionary much as corporate identity had been earlier, but then the brand word got hi-jacked! The new buzz approach from design agencies by the 1980s had become 'we'll design your brand', 'brand by design' etc.

Visual, visual, visual – and it's still largely perceived this way today. We've even seen advertising agencies requested to produce 'brand strategies', but the end result is essentially a tactical campaign, not a brand strategy, because it's based on a graphic approach to brand. We've learned the hard way – you can't build any one element of brand in isolation!

Over these years the world has seen brands come and go just as quickly – Ratners Jewellery chain is a prime example of how a well-known brand can so easily be wrecked by a few unfortunate words.

Škoda on the other hand was the butt of many jokes for years, with a low-class 'a skip on wheels' image, and was eventually taken-over by Volkswagen. The perception of Škoda cars was so poor that Volkswagen had to pour millions of pounds into developing a quality production model, revamping both the internal and external perceptions of the product before they could turn it round and achieve 'Car of the Year' recognition. The point is? Allowing a brand to go wrong is very costly to put right, if in fact you can still do it without being taken over or going into liquidation. So we learnt that brand is not something you create or design then file away as a finished project, or leave it to its own devices – you have to nurture it, develop it, and you have to maintain it. Brand is holistic,[1] but that concept of brand is still nebulous, ill-defined territory.

This is where Phil comes in. While Alan had been primarily visual-based, Phil was honing his IT and web skills, then moving into the high-level management skills required for large financial projects. Witnessing at first hand the gulf between the marketing departments' output to the public, and the internal policies, culture and values of the parent organisations, he began to understand the other side of brand – the non-visual side. This is the area of brand that the

[1] 'Characterised by comprehension of the parts of something as intimately interconnected and explicable only by reference to the whole'.

consumer may not necessarily see, but it's just as vital to get right – as we'll explain later on. Phil came to the conclusion that there were serious disconnects happening that affected the organisational performance – but of course, he had one half the picture, while Alan had the other half!

It was putting these two halves together that filled in the hole that had been dug for the 'brand' word. Brand is not the exclusive servant of Consumer-facing businesses; it is just as essential for small businesses as for large and product-focused businesses that sell to other businesses. It's not simply visual, nor is it subservient to a marketing strategy, or any other area of business. If you still think of brand as primarily visual, then you'll tend to think in terms of B2C marketing, and like many people, miss the real value of holistic branding.

A great example of how to change customer experience and perceptions is the Volkswagen Commercial Vehicle brand. Around 1985 Volkswagen decided to revitalise its existing retailer network and separate the commercial vehicle element from the Volkswagen passenger car franchises. Vans were seen by retailers as the poor man's relation to cars, and marketed in much the same way – only much worse. The product was reliable and known for quality, but the way the products were supported was extremely poor. Anyone wanting to buy a van was directed 'round the back' to the sales office, which was invariably a Portacabin hidden in some corner away from the posh car showroom. No one then had a dedicated team specialising only in commercial vehicles, or anything worth calling a commercially-focused network.

Since then Volkswagen has developed a style and culture that clearly separates the van network from the car retailers. Eventually retailers cottoned on to the fact that running a dedicated Van Centre was actually worth doing, and a completely different approach to business was required from their previous car experience. Specialist van centres were created, many on new sites because van users are far more business-oriented than car customers. A van is a tool of business whether it's a one-man-band or a large fleet carrier, and all businesses demand a high level of product support and customer care.

This has now progressed to a point where the Commercial Vehicles brand is seen by many as the flagship brand in the Volkswagen Group, but there is always work to do, because a brand constantly needs managing. Changes in perceptions, changes in the market, changes in procedures and processes, both in the wider network and within the manufacturer's headquarters, personnel changes at board level, and at trainee level — all potentially affect the brand in innumerable ways on a daily basis.

The starting place is **not** your advertising and marketing

We've also assisted other companies facing potential take-over situations by repairing their brand sufficiently to avoid being subsumed within the larger organisation, together with the inevitable job losses that take-overs always bring. A strong brand is nearly always worth keeping. Mergers and acquisitions involve, and therefore affect, the cultures of the organisations involved — and which one will survive? The strongest! The good news is you don't have to wait (in fact you shouldn't wait) until your company has reached a plateau, or worse, is in decline before getting to grips with building and maintaining a cohesive brand strategy.

Underlying all this is one fundamental issue that we'll address in more detail later — vision. Unless the MD, CEO or proprietor of the business really catches the vision that brand is so vital in the life of their business, the best that will happen is that they will have the building blocks, but never see the wall built. The concept of brand will remain just that – a concept. The starting place of building a healthy, vibrant brand is to envision your team – not revamping your advertising and marketing activities.

So our experience has been wide and long, and as we journeyed, we developed our understanding of brand until we reached the conclusion that, actually, we now understand a lot more about what it really means than we've let on.

Broadly speaking, it appears that no-one yet has really addressed the pressing need of teaching the B2B sector the value of a strong brand, why it works or how to put it into practice. That's the reason for this book. We want you to understand how a holistic brand can really benefit your organisation – whatever size it is, and whatever you do.

Chapter 1
The holistic brand

Many books that deal with the subject of branding will talk about the origins of the word 'brand' and its journey into the modern psyche. They will talk of Norse men, of personalised animals and of soap powder. They will pay homage at the court of the 20th century mega-brands — Nike, BA, GE and Virgin, and they will wax lyrical about the mysteries of corporate identity. Just get your image right and you could be the next Coca-Cola!

In this book we will break through some of the myths that have grown up around the subject of branding. We will demonstrate that branding, as an activity, is not solely the province of large conglomerates or global corporations. We will assert that it is as imperative for SMEs in the B2B sector to get their branding right as it is for the big boys. Finally we will help you, as a small business, to build, manage and sustain your brand so that it becomes a tangible asset in your business that delivers real bottom line benefit.

Great branding is not a mystery, it doesn't take a PHD in rocket science and it needn't cost the earth. That's not to say that it's easy; actually quite the reverse. The difficulties though don't lie in complexity, but in the ability to show dogged determination and single mindedness in driving the business forward with one value-set, one purpose and one direction. Great brands are built by business leaders who take hold of their responsibilities to deliver on the brand promises that their business makes and who refuse to abdicate responsibility for their brand to people who are not empowered or equipped to build it!

A little bit of history

Branding in its modern sense had its origins in the 19th century. With the industrial revolution came mass production. Goods that were traditionally produced locally were now being manufactured centrally and shipped around the country. Manufacturers needed to convince consumers that their goods were not only comparable in quality but, thanks to the introduction of quality control as a by-product of mass production, they were usually better. The need for a consistent look for products became paramount. If it looks the same, it will taste the same, smell the same and perform in the same way. In the early days then, packaging and product were pre-eminent as a means of building customer trust.

In the 1900s, trademark advertising began to gain ground and by the 1940s companies rapidly adopted jingles and slogans as they began to exploit the growing Radio and then TV advertising opportunities. Advertising in mass media began to build the phenomenon of brand recognition as people associated products with tunes, images and snappy strap-lines — triggered by familiar packaging.

The 1960s saw the birth of corporate identity. No longer was it enough to have a differentiated product, it was time to differentiate the company. As the early magic of mass advertising began to become commonplace, the need to engender trust in the company itself became the way to deliver brand. Company logos, styles and strap-lines became de rigueur leading inevitably to the concept of brand equity. Suddenly companies were being bought and sold for far more than their paper value as the brand itself became a marketable asset.

Now is the time for branding to evolve further. In the global, web-enabled, crowded place that is 21st century B2B trading, where

SMEs are in the ascendance, we can no longer rely on a product-based, visually-led view of branding to be sufficient to 'achieve stand-out' as the design world of the late 20th century would put it. It's time to take a long hard look at the world and take a view of branding that fits the landscape. So let's start by looking at brand itself; what it isn't and what it is.

What brand isn't

Brand isn't visual identity. There is a lot of bunkum spoken about brand. Many design agencies offer 'full service branding'. This usually means that they will create a logo, stationery set and, if you're lucky, a brand style guide. They will take your money, pat you on the head and send you off to enjoy your new 'branded' status.

> Will the exercise impress your network?
> **Certainly, but so what?**
>
> Will it lead to more business?
> **Maybe, but on its own it probably won't.**
>
> Will you have a brand?
> **No — you'll have a visual identity.**

Visual identity is a vitally important element of brand, and no brand will survive for long without a well-designed identity. But what a great identity does is to act as a trigger that allows pre-existing perceptions, understanding and trust to be recalled. The key word here is pre-existing. The real work of branding is to build and manage those perceptions, that understanding and that trust. Visual identity in and of itself can never create anything more than subjective opinion. The problem with this is that subjective opinions are transient, fragile and very often wrong.

In this context, the Wikipedia definition of brand as 'a symbolic embodiment of all the information connected to the product and serves to create associations and expectations around it.' works much better if we replace the word 'brand' with the words 'visual identity'. Your visual identity is a tool. Used carefully, it will enhance the effectiveness of your brand. Just don't get seduced into thinking that on its own it is your brand. So step away from the crayons – stop thinking visually for a moment and let's get to the heart of the matter.

stop
thinking visually
for a moment

Brand isn't just a marketing function. In most large corporates, the branding function is left fairly and squarely in the hands of the marketing department. It is commonplace to hear of 'this year's brand strategy'. What is called strategy though is often just another way of describing the latest marketing campaign. The unfortunate truth is that, in so many organisations, brand has become so completely subsumed into the marketing mix, and focus has become so concentrated on the business/client interface, that any thoughts of the wider implications of brand are lost.

When we lump marketing and branding together as though they are subsets of the same activity, the end result is that both activities become devalued. Marketing is largely, by definition, a tactical activity. Tactical marketing is an essential activity if businesses are to take advantage of market conditions. Rapid action based on sound market research is the key to effective marketing activity. This tactical activity should happen within the framework of wider strategic brand considerations. It should be *guided* by the brand; it should not try to *be* the guide.

logo

company name

advertising

products and prices

support literature

research & development

supply chain

customer support

culture

production

human resources

processes

finance

customer relations

delivery

product support

call centres

sales

training

So why does it matter? Welcome to the real world of business in the UK. This is the world where only 0.1% of an estimated 4.5 million businesses[1] fall into the 'large'[2] category. For the other 99.9% the need for intelligent, holistic branding is pressing. The necessity for SMEs to build clear, compelling and robust brands in order to lift themselves above the 'more of the same' brigade is greater now than at any time since the invention of corporate identity in the '60s. This is the world where quality, reliability and service are taken for granted. This is the world where marketing alone is not sufficient to build a loyal customer base. Something more is needed, and that is a holistic brand.

94%

agree that the asset offering the greatest protection during an economic downturn is a strong brand

Finally, brand is not a mystery — we will show you here how you can build, develop and sustain your own brand. It's not always costly, unless of course you get it very wrong — then it can cost a great deal to get it back on track. Brand is not out of reach for the average SME — in fact, by applying the methods we will set out, you too can have a top-class brand that will help you to build and maintain a successful business.

So just what is a brand?

The traditional view that it is a graphical representation of a product or company just won't do any more. Research shows that as little as 15% of any brand is 'visual' like an oil rig, whose impressive superstructure belies the activity beneath. The 'business end' is many hundreds or even thousands of metres below the surface. Indeed, to take a purely visual approach to branding in the B2B sector would, we suggest, be an expensive waste of time, effort and resources. More importantly

[1]   *Source: Department for Business, Enterprise and Regulatory Reform. August 2007*

[2]   *250 or more employees*

it doesn't offer the edge that is required in an increasingly crowded marketplace. It's no longer enough to just stand out in the crowd. To succeed in the 21st century, business must build long-term relationships with customers who return time and again. The brand rubber really hits the road after the first sale is made.

Brand is: 'The culmination of a person's total experience of your organisation, good or bad. It is the effect on your stakeholders of all that your company says and does.'

So brand is dynamic. Brand lives in the mind of your customer, your staff member and your shareholder. Brand is only truly yours when you take time to build, develop and manage it. Branding is about spending time below the waterline, positioning and maintaining the culture of a business. Branding is a lifetime activity.

Where does brand live?

Traditionally, branding has been seen as a marketing function. Because it has been limited to visuals, the focus within most organisations is on the 'above-the-waterline' stuff, much of which is strongly linked to strategic marketing activity. Given that 85% of brand is under the water however, there is a strong case for re-evaluating the status quo. Quality, service, efficiency, sales effectiveness et al. are certainly not marketing activities but belong firmly in the boardroom. This is the realm of strategy and long-term thinking.

An independent survey undertaken by Mori[3] amongst senior board directors of the UK's leading companies concluded that '94% agree that the asset which offers the greatest protection during an economic downturn is a strong brand' whilst 'less than a third feel that their brand offers them a great deal of protection'. This shows that a majority of

---

[3] *Companies selected from the top UK 500 by turnover, the FTSE top 100*
    and the top 100 by capital employed.

successful business leaders understand the value of their brand as a strategic business asset – far more than it is a surface level tactical tool. What most business leaders understand instinctively (even though many don't capitalise on that knowledge) is that to build a brand takes perseverance, effort and focus *in the boardroom*. It's when the strategy, direction and cultural references are clear that brand implementation can happen throughout the organisation. In the rest of this chapter, we will explore some of these strategic reference points and show how these elements can be drawn together to form the basis of brand.

Experience is king

Given that great brand is a culmination of a person's total experience of your organisation, it is vital that the business leader has a clear understanding of where each experience opportunity exists. At its heart, branding is about experience management. If the basis of business is to attract new customers and keep existing ones, perhaps Chief Experience Officer would be a more accurate description of the CEO's role. The traditional model of branding is a two-dimensional, linear one where the focus is firmly restricted to the interface between company and customer.

The real picture though is neither two-dimensional nor linear. There are numerous interfaces with any organisation. What is important is that all of them are managed because each one of them is an opportunity to create an experience that will either enhance and strengthen the brand or damage and weaken it.

So what is 'experience management'? If we accept the concept of touch-points, then it's easy to see that each touch point can and does occur in different areas of the organisation. Connections with customers happen in sales, marketing, customer service and finance.

brand

is the culmination of a person's total experience of your organisation, good or bad. It is the effect on your stakeholders of all that your company says and does.

Connections with suppliers may only be in the purchasing department whilst shareholders will be more likely to interact with the Finance Director's office. The role of the organisation is not to react to these connections, but rather to create brand-led experiences so that each connection is leading the stake-holder into a managed relationship. To build and strengthen the brand, the experience needs to be created *before* it happens.

The people involved in the interaction create each experience individually. The role of the board is to create and lead a culture in which those experiences naturally combine to build trust in the brand at *every level.* Culture is the key element to creating brand-building experiences. Let's look at a common example – the customer service call centre. If the culture in the call centre is one that is driven by targets and scripts, and if employees are constantly worried about being pulled up over very small changes in performance statistics, then what are the likely outcomes?

- Off script issues will not be dealt with satisfactorily.
- Employees will be more focused on achieving targets than on providing excellent service.
- Increased likelihood of customer dissatisfaction.

If, however, the culture in the organisation is one of targets and scripts, but with a primary emphasis on ensuring that each customer's needs are fully met, then the outcomes will be very different.

- A willingness to go off script to meet customer needs.
- Employees, empowered to provide real service, will be more motivated and more productive.
- High levels of customer satisfaction leading to increased retention.

Strategic Partners

Customers

Staff

Press — **Company** — Suppliers

Competition

Network

Shareholders

It's not that targets and scripts are in themselves destructive, it's a matter of emphasis. All businesses need targets, goals, and controls — some need them more than others. These things only become a negative brand influence when the culture within which they are implemented is created around, and focused on, the controls. It's far better to create a culture that empowers everybody in the organisation to deliver great service first. Careful use of metrics and controls in this environment will strengthen the culture, enhance performance and ultimately build a brand that becomes an asset.

First sale, second sale

It costs somewhere between 4 and 7 times more to gain a new client than it does to keep an existing one. Most of us recognise and accept this figure, but have we stopped to ask why this should be? What are the factors that make new clients so much more expensive to acquire and how does brand management influence client retention?

imagine a
football stadium

Attracting new customers requires intensive communication techniques. Firstly, you have to go and find them. They're not going to come to you. When you do find them, you won't have their undivided attention and you won't have them to yourself. Imagine a football stadium. The pitch is full of ordinary people, just milling around, maybe interacting with each other. In the stands, company representatives are shouting about their products. Waving placards and blowing whistles, each one is trying to be noticed by the people on the pitch. The sound is deafening and it's pretty close to impossible trying to hear one voice above the others. In the centre of this crowded stand is you. You shout along and wave your placard.

Sometimes you think you've caught someone's eye down on the pitch, but it's fleeting. The thing is that most of the people on the pitch have no idea who you are. They don't even know that they need your product. They are not looking for you, they are just 'there'.

After a while you start to notice that some areas in the stands are different. Some people are wearing really bright colours. Others have a much bigger placard than their neighbours. Some are shouting into megaphones. There are even some areas where many people have the same placard and are shouting the same thing. One enterprising character has even managed to hack in to the scoreboard and is displaying his messages there. You realise that these people are standing out from the crowd. They have managed to gain a tactical advantage by putting more effort into their 'presentation'. They have spent more money on their outfit. They have spent more money getting themselves a bigger placard. They have sent more people to the stadium. Each one of them has invested more time, more effort, more resource and more money. Even with this advantage though, they still need to shout. They are still surrounded by competitors. The people on the pitch may not be interested in what they have to say.

Finally you manage to attract someone's attention. They beckon you down to the pitch and invite you to tell them all about your product. You now have the daunting task of helping your new friend to understand your product and how it can help them. Answering their difficult questions – why is yours better than all the others? Why should I trust you? It costs *how* much?

Once you have won your customer, the task becomes different. Your purpose now is to deliver. Your product or service now has to live up to the promises you made to attract the client in the first place. Your delivery team needs to deliver what the sales team said it would!

Your service staff must now be the consistent face of the company as they deal with customer queries or problems. In short, your whole organisation must work together to build and sustain a relationship with your client.

Customers don't stay because they love the quality of your advertising. They don't stay because you have a really 'stand-out' logo or a clever strap line. They won't even stay because your product brochure is of the very highest standard. They stay because they are happy with the experience they have had of the organisation. They stay because the product matches the promise. They stay because their questions were answered and their issues were dealt with. Marketing is about attracting your customers in the first place — branding is about keeping them.

So, retention is vital — without retention, growth is both hard work and expensive. Get your retention right and there is a pleasing side effect. The more customers you can retain, the more you will attract. If you want to get more new clients, then a good place to start is to work on keeping your existing ones. Why? Because companies that are good at building relationships that last care about their clients, and companies that care about their clients attract new clients

marketing is about

attracting

your customers

more easily. Back to the stadium — some of those people milling about will be your clients. As they interact with people they come in to contact with, they will be telling their story. Other people who may not have noticed you will be looking out for you because of those stories.

Many businesses find themselves in the uncomfortable position of losing existing customers as fast, if not faster, than they can attract new ones. It's like inviting people into your house through the front door only to have them look around, decide they don't like the décor and leave through the back door. The response from many organisations to this problem is to throw more money at marketing. Getting them in faster, however, won't mean that they'll stay any longer. The challenge is to redress the balance so that customer churn is managed and maintained at a level that is applicable to the market sector.

So our challenge to you, the business leader, is this:

Will you
- create and model an empowered culture?
- focus on building experience before it's happened?
- ensure that your brand grows with every interaction?

branding is about
keeping
them

Chapter 2
Defining your brand

An important part of the branding process is to articulate your brand and what it means to you, and to your stakeholders. The process of describing the brand is the first step to building a brand lexicon that over time will become incorporated within conversation at all levels of the business. Any brand only truly becomes holistic when it has permeated the thought and speech patterns of the business such that the day-to-day behaviours of the organisation are at one with the brand. This becomes the tipping point when the 'effect of all that the business says and does' becomes a powerful outworking of the brand. It's when it starts working for you.

Having understood the concept of the holistic brand and its implications on your business, how do you set about defining your brand? In approaching this question, it is helpful to personalise your brand. The model described in this chapter will help in the process of defining each component of your brand. This is an important first step in the development of a brand strategy. The model allows you to articulate brand attributes so that they may be used across the organisation to inform and drive planning and decision-making.

As can be seen from the diagram, brand can be said to have four aspects. These four elements of brand are: Character, Personality, Talents and Voice. In the rest of this chapter, we will expand on each of these elements and help you to define the parts of your business that make up each element.

The individual elements described here effectively form a cross section of the life of the business. They touch every level — from the boardroom to the shop floor. In describing the brand it is vital to do it in a way that is accessible at all levels of the business. The ideal position is to create an environment in the organisation where anyone in the business, from CEO to delivery driver, is able to describe the brand and how it affects them and their day-to-day work. Individuals need to understand their part in the brand – how every action helps or hinders the journey. A well-defined brand is a vital tool in communicating vision, values and purpose to all areas of the business.

Whilst none of the four elements is more important than any other in terms of the complete brand, the best place to start is with character. Character is the bedrock of brand – it is the base upon which the whole is built.

Character

Character is at the heart of any organisation, just as it is for any individual. Character is what the organisation holds dear; its core vision, its core values, and its core purpose, and is shaped from every response to success or failure from venture formation through to the present. There will have been important drivers behind those decisions that were based on previously held values, presuppositions and 'gut feel'. These drivers – such as fear – may have been a major contributor for pushing a company down one path. Fear of failure, fear of the unknown, or fear of growing too quickly are common business drivers, whilst a strong 'can do' mentality will have driven it along a completely different route. Neither is necessarily right or wrong – it is the way character is formed, and that's why understanding the organisation's character before anything else is so vital.

Here we discover the things that build together to define the character of the organisation. Its history, its differentiators and its fundamental Vision, Values, and Purpose: 'Who are we?' 'Where are we going?' and 'Why does it matter?'

History

Every company has its own history. That history forms a thread that runs through the life of the company. The thread is made up of three different strands, which become intertwined until each becomes an integral part of the whole. The three strands are:

Company time-line – the things that have happened within the business over its life. These events are confined to the life of the business and are specific to it. They will include significant achievements and milestones as well as mistakes and failures. They are often used to mark the company's growth or decline and each event can be viewed as a point on a graph.

CHARACTER

Assimilated histories − each time a person joins a company, they bring with them a personal history, a set of events that make up their own personal timeline. The same is true where companies expand by acquisition. Each new addition will bring its own timeline and assimilated histories to the party. Whilst these assimilated histories will not be specifically visible on the company time-line, they will certainly influence the history that is being created. Any business is what it is as a result of where it has come from, and the collective histories of all of its people.

Mythology − a set of popular beliefs or assumptions about the company that form over time. As the history of the business forms and unfolds, there exists the opportunity for myths to be created. Half remembered events, stories that have been embellished and exaggerated over years become part of the corporate 'story'. It is possible to create a positive mythology within the culture of an organisation. It can indeed be a very powerful tool that can be used both to inspire new and existing staff, and to encourage improved performance. It's important to state that creating a mythology is not about making stories up, creating successes that didn't happen or hiding mistakes. Rather it is about creating a set of stories that together form a positive mythology.

The best way to gain advantage from the history of a business is to recognise all of it. It is important to celebrate achievements, to learn from mistakes (publicly if necessary) and to use each of these to build a positive mythology that surrounds the business. In marketing terms, the power of stories is hard to overstate. People relate to stories − it's part of the way we are. The business that is able to use their history to create a set of stories that can be used in a wide range of contexts has a very powerful tool. Stories can be used in the sales process to demonstrate expertise and authority in a way that is more memorable and impactful than a straightforward presentation of products. People want to hear how the company has helped others like them to overcome their problems far more than to be taken through an endless list of product features. They can also be extremely helpful when inducting new employees into the culture of the company, giving them a sense of belonging and integration.

Differentiators

Many businesses never ask themselves the question 'why does it matter?' and yet it is fundamental to the survival and growth of the business. Why does it matter that this or that company exists? What is it that people would not be able to get if the company ceased to be? This is not differentiation at the product level – it's not a question of features and benefits. This is the differentiation between companies in terms of the whole package. It's about understanding why clients choose to build a long-term relationship with the organisation. Why people are attracted to working in that organisation and why they want to stay. Why suppliers choose to build lasting relationships. It's what makes you the supplier of choice, the client of choice or the employer of choice.

These fundamental differentiators are powerful tools in the brand strategy process. They can be used internally to encourage and envision staff. They are very powerful motivators when building internal culture because they can generate a drive to strengthen differentiators and widen gaps between organisations. They are also invaluable when building a set of core messages that can be used to build and inform marketing strategy.

Differentiators should be constantly reviewed, tested and managed if they are to keep their positive influence. It really doesn't pay to get complacent with your core differences – don't assume that because you had the best all round offering last year that you do this year. Research is vital. Test the competitors, ask your clients, know the environment and get feedback from your staff.

Values

When did you last articulate your company values? Do you know what they are? If you asked members of your staff would they be able to tell you? Values underpin your character. They form the basis upon which the future of the organisation is mapped out. They exist to inform and influence decision making across the organisation. Values will dictate the way that a company responds to crisis and will be the guiding principles that shape the culture.

values are about articulating company character

Values are a tool to describe the way that the organisation behaves. They are not primarily aspirational, attempting to describe a company that we would like to be. Values are about articulating company character. They are non-negotiable. Where there is an aspirational element to company values, it is in creating a culture in which adherence to, and exhibiting of, values is recognised and applauded.

Successful businesses are crystal clear about their values – and they live them out. The role of the board in this area is key. They must drive the internal communication of values. They must find ways to induct new staff into the values and culture of the company. Most importantly, they must model the values themselves. It may be a truism, but values live when values are lived. In other words, if values are to have a positive impact on the life and success of the business, they must be lived out in every area of the business.

Vision

Vision is a widely misunderstood concept in business. Vision is often used as a kind of pie in the sky statement of hope that carries with it an air of desperation. It's as if by saying 'We will be this' or 'We will increase profitability by that' then somehow these things will happen. The other extreme is that companies create vision statements that are little more than a list of the things they currently do. The latter of course being the easiest to achieve because they are doing it already! Of course, there are all shades in between.

Vision as a tool in business should drive growth. It should provide direction and be used as a measure for strategic decision making. It should act as an inspiration to push a company on to greater achievement and, at its best, it becomes a cultural marker that works to create an environment of success. Vision is the banner that is planted at the centre of the battlefield to rally the troops and provide a focal point for the 'action' of the business.

Great vision doesn't just say 'this is what we hope for the future', it says 'this is what we believe about this company, this is what we value, this is what we are here for, this is where we are headed and this is how we are going to get there'. So as well as laying out the values of the company, an important consideration is to identify the purpose of the company.

Purpose is the answer to the question 'what are we here for?' or 'what do we exist to do?' Your purpose could be to help businesses to create better business plans, or it could be to help reduce global warming by providing affordable business recycling services. The crucial thing is that your purpose is not 'to make more money' — that's an outcome, not a purpose. Your purpose is a statement of what you do. Get this right and it will repay you in spadefuls. It will be a driver for your sales team. It will inform your marketing and it will form the basis of your staff development programme. Identifying and communicating clear purpose brings clarity to all of your business activities.

Vision also talks about the future — where we are headed. A valuable exercise for any organisation is to determine a long-term goal. By long-term we mean 20, 30, 50 years. A big goal, a difficult goal, an inspiring goal. This is the long-term direction of the company. It's like planting a flag on the far horizon. It's always visible in the distance and it provides a marker to keep the company moving in the right direction. A long-term goal allows a business to test its 3 or 5 year business. Having written the big goal it becomes the compass for the journey and each step can be tested against the criteria 'does this take us towards our goal or not?' allowing focus to be retained.

It's no good though just to have a big goal. A key to completing a vision statement is to talk about the next step. What small steps does the company need to take now to move towards the goal? This part of the vision statement is like the earth wire that keeps the whole thing grounded. A good vision statement is one that has an immediate impact on every area of company life. It's not just about dreaming, it's about doing something now to achieve the dream. In chapter 3 we will discuss how to structure a vision statement and how to incorporate it within an overall brand strategy.

Personality

Unlike character which remains fairly static, the personality is much more likely to adjust and change over time. Personality in the context of brand definition is about what the company is like. It's how your staff define the company they work for and how your customers describe the company they buy from. A company's personality will influence the way that it communicates with all of its stakeholders. It will affect the culture or 'feel' of a company and consequently will have a bearing on issues such as morale and productivity.

persona(:ty

In many ways the personality of the company will be a major factor for potential customers when deciding whether to do business with the organisation.

It's common for each of us to decide whether to do business with, or get involved with, someone on the basis of feelings. Gut feelings and first impressions are very often the over-riding factor in business decisions. Indeed many of the most successful business people and entrepreneurs will attribute much of their success to 'trusting their gut'. It would be nice to think that our potential clients make their buying decisions based on cold logic and hard figures; alas the reverse is more often true. The astute business leader then will be aware of, and will manage, organisational personality so that there is a fit between business and target audience.

Some of the things that combine to create organisational personality are likes and dislikes, beliefs, opinions, environment and people. 'what are we like?' and 'how do we behave?'

Likes and dislikes
Organisations are made up of people, and just as people all have likes and dislikes, so organisations have likes and dislikes. A start-up business will display the preferences of the founder and as the organisation grows, it will inherit the preferences of those that join it. Over time, a set of corporate likes and dislikes will evolve that will become a part of the culture of the organisation and will influence the way that it does business.

So, for example, if the business founder dislikes 'hard sell' techniques in the sales process, then the organisation my well evolve a sales structure that is more focused on 'soft selling'.

---

38   [1]   *Endless Referrals: Network Your Everyday Contacts Into Sales –*
              McGraw-Hill 1998

**ALL THINGS BEING EQUAL
PEOPLE DO BUSINESS WITH**

**AND GIVE REFERRALS TO PEOPLE
THEY KNOW, LIKE AND TRUST**

Bob Burg[1]

That may be a good thing or a bad thing; it is not our intention to make a judgement. It is important however to understand, especially in a mature business, those things which have influenced the behaviours that are being exhibited in the organisation.

Often businesses fail to perform to their potential because they behave in a way that has become the norm within their culture. Such behaviours may well stem from deep-seated preferences within the organisation. When it comes to building and maintaining a corporate culture, understanding the organisational preferences is an extremely helpful thing.

There are different types of likes and dislikes to address when building a brand strategy. Some preferences involve higher-level decision making, and the choices will have to support the vision, values and purpose, as they have to do with the type, size and quantity of work undertaken. For example, what does the organisation's board prefer – small clients or large clients (both have inherent challenges)? What spread of customer base – few or many, high-volume with low-value work, or low-volume with high-value work? Do they prefer vertical markets (such as telecommunications) or a broad spectrum of client markets? These are not just questions of good business planning, they are also integral to how the brand strategy will be built later. After all, there's not much point in trying to build a customer base that is at odds with your preferences any more than trying to create a funky modern brand culture, if all the machinery is thirty years old and the youngest member of the team is nearing retirement!

Some of these questions will already have been answered of course, but it pays to revisit likes and dislikes to ascertain not only what is profitable, but what people enjoy working on the most, how they can achieve difference and what they would most like to expand into.

There are another set of likes and dislikes that deal with internal culture. Although this set of questions involves HR policies, they are not the sole remit of the personnel people. Everyone has their own pet hates and personal tastes – but unless an organisation can override these and build a culture that is clearly defined and carefully managed, they risk alienation of one group or another, even over things like dress codes, messy desks, boring workspaces or the level of communication. Although these likes and dislikes can be particularly noticeable in smaller SMEs, the same issues are encountered in multinationals – there are just more people in the organisation, and the vast majority of the workforce has not been involved in building the culture that exists. Herein lies a truth about culture; you cannot impose a culture on a group of people – they will form their own. Thus if it is necessary to change an internal culture, the only sure fire way to succeed is through collaboration. Organisations that neglect the culture issue will find they could develop a negative culture very quickly, and it will always be founded on unresolved issues, bad communication, or lack of involvement. This is not to say that once you have decided upon a culture that it is open to be influenced by every new employee that joins. Quite the opposite! There is a distinct difference between culture, and company rules that need to be imposed. It's clear that culture must be well managed, but it must also be built in as an integral part of a clearly defined brand strategy.

Well-managed cultures have a common internal belief system about the company that is shared by everyone, creating an environment that everyone can buy into – even before the offer of employment. A positive internal culture will often be communicated by employees to the customers subconsciously, as well as through any policy guidelines, and where there is a culture that allows people to think outside the box to resolve Customer Relation Management issues (CRM), the reputation of the brand will be protected if things occasionally 'go wrong'.

Beliefs and opinions

Within any organisation, there will exist a set of beliefs. These will include beliefs about the company, about the marketplace and about the competition. What we believe about our abilities and ourselves will influence the way that we behave and will ultimately affect our success. Collective self-confidence is a huge factor in becoming a successful business and is something that should be encouraged and nurtured.

When it comes to driving the vision of the company, there is a requirement for single mindedness especially in the area of corporate self-belief. Without exception, the most successful businesses have a sense of belief in themselves and what they are doing that is unshakeable. This can often be misinterpreted as arrogance; it is actually nothing of the sort. If we don't believe in what we are doing — why would anyone else? Self-belief leads to passion and when we are able to communicate with passion, people take notice. Passion is infectious. A conversation with a passionate person leaves us energised, envisioned and positive.

Interestingly, what we believe is not always the same as what is true. Self-belief on its own for example does not guarantee success; it is merely part of the picture. Many companies suffer from a belief that their competitors are stronger or more well positioned than they are. It is very common for staff to have less belief in the organisation than the business owners or leadership team. Corporate belief systems need managing. The job of the CEO is to align internal belief with brand reality to build passionate ambassadors for the brand.

Identifying, articulating and where necessary, debunking corporate belief systems then are an integral part of defining a brand. It is imperative that the brand building process should include time

Don't
let the opinions
of the average man
sway you... Dream, and
he thinks you're crazy
Succeed, and he thinks
you're lucky. Acquire
wealth, and he
thinks you're
greedy. Pay no
attention
He simply

DOESN'T
UNDER
STAND

Robert G Allen

and effort spent on these activities so that as culture is built, beliefs are matched to the corporate vision. It's all well and good having a corporate vision, but if there is a general disbelief about its achievability, then it will almost certainly fail.

Environment

Environment feeds culture; culture feeds performance, and performance feeds success. The operating environment for the business is crucial. Why? Because whilst your marketing feeds a set of massages to your marketplace, the way that you develop your operating environment speaks volumes internally. Companies that use their workspace to motivate and encourage employees not only get a more productive workforce, but also will maximise the potential of communicating core messages such as the vision, values and purpose.

It's also necessary to understand the commercial environment in which you operate. Close monitoring of market trends is a discipline that can be easily overlooked in the day-to-day business of running the company. Look what happened to Sony when they failed to keep up with technology. Apple stole a march on them with the iPod that they may never recover. Sony moved from a position as market leader, with their Walkman range, to playing catch-up with Apple. At best, Sony's perceived position now is that of being in the chasing pack. That's an expensive mistake for a very large company to make. Keeping up with what's happening in the big wide world is crucial for maintaining brand position in an ever-changing marketplace.

Of course, the word environment is connected most often with green issues. Ask the man in the street what is meant by environment and most will use words like global-warming, carbon footprint and greenhouse gasses. Many larger organisations now take Corporate

Social Responsibility (CSR) very seriously. There is an expectation from the buying public that large corporations should 'put something back'. CSR is fast becoming a fundamental part of operating a modern organisation. Of course CSR isn't just about managing emissions or minimising waste. Having an involvement, and an input into, the communities in which we do business is a powerful way to communicate corporate interest and generate brand awareness and respect.

Discussions about environment become a core part of brand strategy because from whichever viewpoint, environment communicates personality. Whether physical, corporate or local, the way that an organisation connects to and manages its environment projects a sense of what the organisation is like that will be picked up by potential customers, staff, shareholders and suppliers in an incredibly powerful way.

People

In many ways, your people are your business. People do business with people, not with companies. The only way that your brand can permeate your organisation is by becoming a part of the collective psyche of the business. This transition from theory to practice happens at a people level. It's when employees get involved with the direction and vision of the company, such that it becomes 'their' company and 'their' vision that brand magic really happens.

What this means to the organisation is that it is imperative that the brand is effectively communicated to staff. Communication here is not about putting a page in the staff handbook or a poster on the wall! This is about holding a conversation with each member of staff, a conversation that starts with the staff induction process and continues through the life of the employment. This kind of dialogue is about reinforcing and connecting the brand values and the vision of the business at every opportunity so that they become a part of the culture. Team briefings, whole company meetings, board meetings, performance appraisals should all include a brand element. The brand forms a framework that drives and informs communication and activity at all stages.

But brand has an impact even earlier in the employment process. Recruitment policy is a key area of business strategy and great care needs to be taken to ensure that all recruitment activity is focused on the brand journey. What does this mean in practical terms? How often does a CV contain the phrase 'works well as part of a team'? Have you ever seen one that doesn't say that? The important question is not will this person work well in a team, rather it is will this person work well in *my* team. It's not just fitting in with a team that's important, it's about finding and recruiting people who will have a positive impact on the company's culture. So when you advertise and interview — how much effort is involved in assessing the cultural fit of the candidate?

your **brand** is irreplaceable

As far as recruitment is concerned, the 80:20 rule applies — 80% attitude, 20% aptitude. The truth is that given a baseline standard of aptitude, skills can be trained, but hire someone who has an attitude that will clash with the culture and you're asking for trouble. It's very hard to train attitude (although not impossible) and it's even harder to fix cultural breakdown caused by employees that don't fit.

In all of this though, it's important to remember one thing. This will be a concept that is contentious for some, and downright outrageous for others! The thing is, your most valuable asset is not your people, it's your brand. The purpose of ensuring that you have the right people, that they are trained and developed in a managed way and that they inhabit a culture that has been designed and built from the top down is to build your brand. Your brand doesn't exist to keep your staff happy and content, your staff are there to keep your brand focused and functioning. That's not to say of course that your people are unimportant – actually the reverse is true. Staff development, managed recruitment and staff welfare are crucial elements of brand management but in the end, any individual in the organisation can be replaced. Your brand is irreplaceable.

Attitude : ● Aptitude

Talents

The talents of the business relate to the skills and products that the company has. Part of understanding and articulating the brand is to be able to define in detail what the product or service is that the business produces. People throughout the business need to be able to describe the product set of your business. In the context of staff as brand advocates, it's not enough for them to only understand what they do as individuals, they should be able to put their contribution into the context of the company offering.

People talk to each other and one of the most commonly asked questions when people first meet is 'what do you do?' This is a golden opportunity for a brand advocate to communicate the purpose of the business. The conversation could go one of two ways:

1. An employee who doesn't really know
   what the business purpose is...

   Friend: 'What do you do?'
   Employee: 'I'm a receptionist'
   Friend: 'Who do you work for?'
   Employee: 'Company X'
   Friend: 'That's interesting, do you have any hobbies?'
2. An employee who understands the company purpose...

   Friend: 'What do you do?'
   Employee: 'I'm a receptionist'
   Friend: 'Who do you work for?'
   Employee: 'Company X – we help business to...'
   Friend: 'That's interesting, how do you do that?'

In the second example, an opportunity has been taken to let someone else know what the purpose of the business is. Who knows where that piece of information will end up – the friend may be the wife of a business owner who is within the company's target market and a

ta1ents

genuine enquiry may have been generated. The key thing here is that when people know what the business does, they will happily say so — when they don't, the conversation will always be focused on their particular role. So part of understanding the product set is to create a simple way for everyone to describe it.

The individual areas covered within talents are products and services, customers, pricing, benefits and value. These areas answer the questions 'what do we do?' and 'what can we do for you'.

Products/Services

As we have said above, it is vital that the output of the organisation — the thing(s) that you are selling — is clearly defined. It is remarkable how few employees in large organisations can articulate what it is that their company does. There is a responsibility on senior management to ensure that product familiarisation is part of the induction process for new staff and that changes and additions to the products or services are communicated to all staff. How often are staff encouraged to visit your own web-site and keep up with the latest product news? The purpose is not to make each member of staff a specialist, just that they understand the product enough to be able to describe to someone how it could help them or their business.

Another reason for having a clear and up-to-date description of the product and/or services is so that you can stay current with industry trends and developments. Periodic research should be undertaken to understand what's new and what the next big thing in your particular sector is likely to be. Back to Sony — failure to predict the move from CD/MiniDisc to MP3 players cost them dear in terms of both market share and reputation. More importantly, they lost a brand foothold. Prior to the introduction of the iPod, personal stereos were beginning to be commonly referred to as 'Walkman' regardless of manufacturer

– that ground has probably been irretrievably lost to Apple. It pays to stay current. Your mistakes may not be as big or as public as Sony's, but they will be just as damaging for you.

Customers

We've all heard the term 'customer centric', it's a common buzz-phrase in use by marketeers and advertisers the world over. The question to be answered is 'how well do we know our customers?'. To be truly customer centric requires detailed and up-to-date knowledge. Many businesses, however, continue to rely on old understanding and assumptions. Old understanding because there is no investment, either of resources or time, in the process of maintaining relationship with existing clients. Assumption because it is common to assume that you know what drives your customers, usually based on a desire to find yet more opportunities to explain the feature list associated with your product or service.

build a profile of your **ideal** customer

Being customer centric means spending time on CRM and here there are no short-cuts. From the very first contact the relationship between customer and company needs to be managed and nurtured. CRM actually starts before the first contact. A clear and carefully constructed customer profile which allows the business to target resource and effort in starting conversations with the right prospects is vital. How much resource is wasted every year having pointless discussions with people who are never going to be converted to customers merely because they were the wrong people to be talking to in the first place? The moral? Build a profile of your ideal customer. Understand them before you ever meet them! What drives them? Who are their ideal customers? How much time, effort and money are they going to invest with you? How does your offering help them to deliver theirs?

In terms of your own brand, who you choose to do business with is very important. When people start to build ideas about what your brand is, they don't just look to the product. They don't just look at the identity and they don't just look at your staff. People need to be reassured that you understand them, their marketplace and their particular business issues. One of the easiest and most accessible ways that people make the judgement about whether or not you are the right organisation to help them is your client list. Do they recognise the names in your portfolio? Do those names resonate in terms of size, sector or client-base? The truth is that people make judgements about you based on all sorts of criteria. The whole thrust of holistic branding is to ensure that you manage those criteria to give your clients and prospects a consistent message and experience whatever the criteria they are choosing to use.

Pricing

Pricing is a very interesting area when it comes to determining, managing and communicating brand. It is critical to the success of the business that the pricing model is right for the product or service in order to remain both competitive and profitable. It is also critical, however, that the pricing model is right for the brand. There is a straightforward two-dimensional model that is often used to determine price strategy. These two dimensions are cost/margin and competition. The cost/margin dimension is simply the cost of manufacture and the cost of sale with the required profit margin added to give a sale price for the product and/or service. The competition element is often the tool used to derive the margin that can be applied. By looking at the marketplace and comparing competitors pricing for similar products a margin can be applied that enables product positioning to be managed.

There is a difficulty with the traditional two-dimensional model. Two-dimensional pricing means by its very nature that competition is often on the basis of cost. In order to remain competitive in a price battle, the temptation is to squeeze the margins. True, there is often opportunity to reduce costs and overheads and introduce efficiencies into the manufacturing process, but when that is done, the only thing left to squeeze is the margin. The net result is often improved market share at the expense of profitability.

It is possible to break out of this cycle. By introducing a third dimension into the pricing strategy, market share can be improved without sacrificing profitability. The magic element? Brand of course. There is a universal rule of business that demand increases as cost decreases. Whilst this is a bit of a generalisation, it is undoubtedly true of most products and services on the market. So demand for a Rolls Royce will be considerably lower than for a Ford Focus. What the application of the third dimension does for pricing strategy is not to fundamentally change that rule, but rather to allow the company to demand a higher price for the product or service before demand begins to fall.

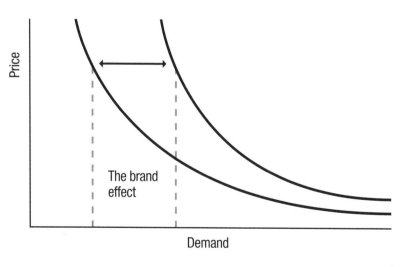

What the introduction of brand considerations does to the buying decision is to take that decision away from the realm of price alone. Importantly, one of the strongest motivating factors in customer retention is not price, it's a satisfying brand experience. Remember the saying 'Nobody ever got fired for buying IBM'? That has nothing to do with price — IBM have never been the cheapest brand. People want to feel confident when they are purchasing. They want to be sure they're not making a mistake. Those motivators are far more complex than just cost.

Benefits

Do you know what the benefits of your product are to your customers and potential customers? How does what you do really help? When did you last ask the question 'what are my customers buying?'. This is a very interesting question that is not necessarily the same as 'what am I selling?'. There is a strong correlation here with the discussion about pricing. Understanding a customer's needs, motives and motivators is vital when making decisions about brand positioning and the messages that surround the brand. If we focus on the product benefits as we perceive them then we will, in all likelihood, miss the point completely.

What is important to the customer is their problem — and that may well not be on the list of problems that we say the product can solve. This is a key area for building a strong brand and the way to ensure that it is right is twofold. Firstly, research your market. There really is no substitute for hard work here — inaccurate assumptions that you make about the needs of current and future customers can be very costly. Spend time with your existing customers finding out why they come to you and not your competitors and what problems your product solves for them. Secondly, make sure that your sales process is tailored to finding out what your prospects issues really are. Re-train the sales staff if necessary. You can be sure that as soon as you start turning the focus of your sales conversations to understanding and solving your prospects problems, your conversion rates will increase dramatically. Only talk about benefits when they are tailored to solving specific and identified problems. Remember — Assumption is the mother of all stuff-ups!

When the product that is supplied meets the real needs of the customer, then the decision question is not one of price, it's one of value. The decision becomes centred around the worth of the product, not the price that is asked for it. Value is about a holistic experience and is not confined to a list of features or a price. Value is about choosing a brand rather than a product. Value is about differentiation on a fundamentally different level than that of product comparison.

you can have your crayons back now!

Voice

The fourth sector of the brand model talks about the voice of the organisation. By voice here we don't mean to narrow the discussion to spoken or written attributes. The voice is really the expression of the way that stakeholders experience the organisation in a sensory way. So it's not just about what is heard, it's also about what is seen. It is very much about how you say what you say and about connecting up all the messages so that, together, they form one coherent message. The voice of the organisation is very often the way that it is initially recognised. In brand speak, this is where we start to talk about the visual identity of the brand. Visual identity is very often what is mistaken for brand and so in many people's minds the two things are synonymous. However, as we have demonstrated, identity without brand is transient, inefficient and very often ineffective.

It is important to remember the other elements of the brand when addressing matters of voice. The voice – or identity – of a brand stands or falls on the effectiveness of the other three parts, namely character, personality and talents. A good, well defined and carefully managed brand provides a platform on which the identity of the business can function as it should, which is as a consistent trigger allowing the beliefs and perceptions of the organisation to be recalled. Interestingly, the identity will act as a negative trigger if the perception of the organisation has been arrived at as a result of poor experiences of the brand. So the identity itself cannot influence perception at any more than a surface level because real perception is a result of experience. Identity can be a good or a bad trigger, by virtue of its quality, uniqueness and consistency, but to expect it to deliver a lasting belief system about the brand is naive and unreasonable.

In this section, we will explore the relationship between the design, delivery, usage and communication of the organisation's identity.

voice

By dealing with each element of voice individually, a checklist can be created that will help to form a brief for the creation of the corporate identity. This has a number of advantages both in terms of articulating the voice, and for briefing creative agencies. An important consideration is that the 'likeableness' of graphic design is entirely subjective. This means that to get the best from designers, a clear brief is essential. Clear, unambiguous briefs are notoriously hard to write — what you think is crystal clear may mean very little to a designer. Anything that helps to make this process more efficient will ease the process and result in a far greater chance of a successful outcome. The key in this process is constant communication. Don't be afraid to ask your agency to reiterate the brief back to you so that you are sure that they are approaching the project from a place of complete understanding.

Tone

You can tell in a conversation what someone's feeling, saying, implying or alluding to by the tone of voice that is being used. At its most simple, this can be illustrated by the way parents communicate with very young children. Interactions will often use tone to communicate an emotion or message far more than the words that are being used. In fact many interactions with babies and toddlers do not include words at all, but depend on a series of made up words or sounds to convey a message that is understood very clearly by the infant. As we grow up, we never lose the ability to draw messages from interactions by paying attention mostly to tone. We know if someone is angry, disappointed, or happy by a number of indicators but one of the most basic is their tone.

This is important for businesses to understand when constructing messages and vehicles for communicating those messages. The audience will, to a greater or lesser degree, be expecting a particular tone of voice in the message based on their perception of the personality of the organisation. It is clear then that care must be taken to ensure that the delivery of the messages is consistent with the personality of the brand. 'What are we like?' needs to be at the forefront of any thinking when designing communication content and delivery. A mismatch here may well put the audience off without them knowing why; it will just 'feel' wrong. Audiences here are both external (clients and prospects) and internal (staff, shareholders etc.) and neither set of communications should be considered without reference to tone.

Colour

Colour is a funny thing. It is possible to use colour to great effect to convey meaning – think about IBM and their use of blue. For many, blue is a symbol of conservative, professional reliability. Red is often associated with immediacy and passion, green with the environment. The list is endless and there are, of course, differing shades of colour and uses of two or more colours together that will complicate the picture. What is at the heart of good colour choice, both for corporate identity and for the delivery of messages is that the choice reflects the character and personality of the brand. It should also be appropriate for the market place in which you operate. Shocking pink, for example, may not be appropriate if you are dealing exclusively with accountants in a male dominated marketplace. Sounds too obvious? It's surprising how many smaller organisations try to be what they're not when it comes to use of colour.

Along with the main colours in the corporate identity, a palette of secondary colours to be used in all areas of communication should be chosen. Web sites, for example, should adhere to the identity rules. What colour background is being used, what colour font is picked for titles or body text? Consistency here will ensure that every page of the site will look professional and will reflect the personality and character of the brand. Likewise, printed materials like trade press advertising, product brochures and staff communications need to display an element of consistency. Where there are noticeable differences in styles, layout and use of colour, messages become lost in the noise and confusion of a plethora of styles and the effectiveness of the message is lessened considerably.

Style

The communication style of a brand is indicative of the personality of the brand. If you want to convey a professional and serious personality, it's not wise to use a lot of pastel or primary colours, or a very informal layout style. Equally, black or dark blue with a very rigid style does not convey a fun or quirky personality. But you can use combinations both of colour and style to convey any number of nuances of personality and character. The important thing is that any choice is intentional and is made with reference to all the other areas of the brand. When this happens, the brand delivery really starts to be holistic in nature.

As has been said before, it is vital for the integrity of the brand that each experience of the brand is consistent. It is also vital that each brand experience reinforces the perceptions that you want to build in the audience. Inconsistent delivery styles are often the cause of the erosion of brand reputation. Consider the case of a manufacturer with a set of badged products. The message that the manufacturer wants to convey is that the product set can and should be used to create a complete solution. If each product is advertised in trade press with a different style and different use of colour, the net result will be that each product is individual and is best used that way. If, however, each product is advertised in a consistently similar style there will be a subliminal message that says 'these products come from the same place, have the same quality of build and functionality and can be used as a family'. The difference in the mind of the audience will be marked. Brand awareness will increase, messages will be assimilated more easily and the brand reputation will be enhanced. For the brand to be really successful now requires the manufacturer to deliver on that promise. The quality of the products must stand up, as must the delivery and service levels, but above all it must be easy to use the product set to create solutions, otherwise all the hard work will be wasted.

Language

How often do you review the language that you use, both internally and externally? Clear and suitable language is essential to good communication. If an organisation really wants to build a holistic brand – one that is effective internally and externally – then the style, tone and level of vocabulary used to communicate with their stakeholders must be complimented by the language of their culture. How you wish to be seen, for example as an established authority in your market, or as highly innovative, or maybe as a fresh new approach, will dictate that choice. Again, the emphasis needs to be on a language style that fits with the character, personality and talents of the brand to ensure consistency of delivery. The concept of a brand lexicon is perhaps a new thought, but in many cases will ensure that communication across the board is clear and unambiguous.

This is often particularly relevant in internal communications. The lexicon of words, terms and phrases can shape the perception of the organisation among the work-force. When the brand is being defined, and a holistic strategy for the brand is being developed, this choice of vocabulary is vital. Messages that are consistent, not only in terms of style, tone and design, but in the choice of language used will be stronger and more effective. Choices made at board level about how to refer to products, services, culture, behaviours and activities will ensure that whatever the source of the message, the language and delivery is consistent.

Rhythm and Volume

This may seem like an odd concept in terms of the identity of an organisation and the delivery of its message, but rhythm and volume are interesting and important aspects of voice. Rhythm in this context is not about the delivery of individual messages – the speed that you talk is not the issue. What is important is that in the development of a holistic brand strategy, the rhythm and pace of the delivery of brand messages is considered and defined. Again, the importance of aligning the frequency of delivery with the character and personality of the brand is very important. What is also vital is to match that rhythm with the expectations of the marketplace. When messages are regular and consistent, they set up a rhythm that over time becomes more like resonance. It's resonance that is the goal when delivering brand messages. Resonance in a mechanical sense is when an object is subjected to a force that has a frequency that is close to its own frequency. Figuratively, resonance is the ability to suggest or evoke images, memories and emotions. So, the aim of rhythm in brand communication – whether internal or external – is to set up that resonance in the audience that enables memories, perceptions and emotions to be triggered. Remember – branding is all about creating an experience – resonance will enhance and remind the audience of those brand experiences.

resonance is **the goal** when delivering brand messages

Volume also has a role to play in creating brand resonance. At its simplest, consistently loud messages will generate reaction faster than more subtle ones. Life, however, is rarely simple and many other factors should be considered when deciding an appropriate volume level for brand communication. If your brand personality is subtle and understated, it won't help to communicate in a loud or brash way.

You will set up a resonance – but it will be more like troops marching across a bridge in step. Eventually it will collapse. An illustration of positive resonance is of running a wet finger around the rim of a crystal wine glass. When you get it right, you can create a clean, pure tone that is impossible to miss. Choose rhythm and volume carefully when considering your brand communications – getting it wrong will cause your message to be discordant and may well destroy the hard work you have put in to delivering the other aspects of the holistic brand strategy.

Message

Having considered the delivery of the brand from the point of view of tone, colour, style, rhythm, volume and language, you are now ready to start to formulate the brand messages. What you say about yourself, your product and the way that you operate is fundamentally important. By now you should have all of the tools necessary to create a core brand message and the best place to start is with the organisation's core purpose. Purpose is the answer to the question 'what are we here for?' and so will be a key element in communicating the brand to all of your audiences. The core message forms the centre from which a selection of messages can be developed. It is the foundational message from which all others spring.

The key to developing supplementary messages is that each one should also make reference to the core message – whether through the use of language i.e. key words or phrases, or through tone and style. In general, ambiguity is not helpful when delivering brand messages. Of course you may devise a marketing campaign that contains some element of ambiguity as a vehicle to attract attention in a new market. These messages are often referred to as 'teasers' and are intended to leave the audience looking for the next message to find out more. In the B2B market, such methods should be used sparingly. In reality, when communicating with busy professionals or business owners, such subtleties are often wasted. So the general rule of thumb is to be simple, consistent and unambiguous when creating your messages.

The same general rule applies to internal brand communications. There is often a very short space of time in which to communicate a message. People's days are crowded and their minds are often crowded too; there is limited opportunity to get that message across. So keep it simple, keep it regular, keep it short and keep it consistent. There is a methodology that teachers use when delivering lessons which says 'tell them what you're going to say, say it and then tell them what you just said'. It's not a bad rule for delivering brand messages either.

Summary

Character, personality, talents and voice — the four fundamentals of brand. By addressing each area separately, we are able to define the brand and create something that is unique to the business. Separation on the basis of visual identity alone, as we have seen, is never going to deliver lasting advantage. Equally, separation on the basis of product, features or price is unlikely to create a unique proposition. But separation on the basis of a well defined, well managed and holistic brand will set the business apart from its competitors. It will build strength and value into the company and will offer protection even in turbulent economic times.

Chapter 3
Building strategy

We have talked about how to define a brand from the fourfold aspects of character, personality, talents and voice. We have shown that the effective brand is one that is holistic — it is one that defines, informs and permeates all areas of the business. Now we turn our attention to the task of building a strategy for the brand that can be used to deliver business benefit in all functional areas of the business. It's not enough to simply define the brand — the brand must be put to work for the business. Without this critical step, all else is expensive vanity. The way to put the brand to work is to develop a brand strategy that can be used across the business in all of its planning activities. This quote sums up strategy beautifully:

> '*Strategy is a style of thinking, a conscious and deliberate process, an intensive implementation system, the science of ensuring future success.*'
>
> Pete Johnson

Strategy is intrinsically linked with success. It is the ability to recognise strengths and weaknesses within the organisation. It is the ability to recognise and forecast environmental change and manage the impact of that change on the organisation. It is about identifying competitors' strengths and weaknesses and exploiting both to gain market advantage. Strategy is about the process of turning an envisioned future into an empowered, tangible reality.

So just how do you go about building a brand strategy? In this chapter, we will introduce the three elements of a holistic brand strategy.

We will look in detail at each part of the strategy and break it down into its constituent parts. Building a brand strategy is not dissimilar to eating an elephant! To attempt a whole one may appear daunting, but in small chunks, it becomes a manageable task.

Holistic brand strategy consists of a journey through three separate areas: The brand manifesto, the brand plan and brand delivery. In fact, the strategy exists as a culmination of work on those three areas – and the delivery of sustainable brand advantage is then a function of great strategy execution.

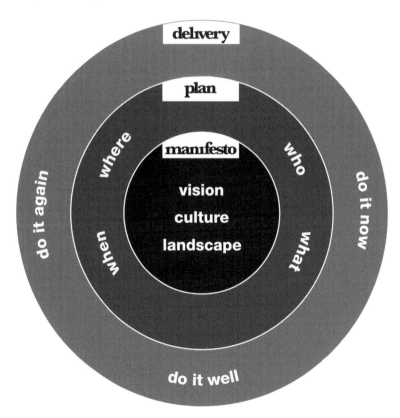

Brand manifesto

A brand manifesto is the first step to building a holistic brand strategy. The manifesto is a definition of the envisioned organisation, its culture and the landscape in which it operates. Let's take a look at each part of the brand manifesto starting with envisioning.

Envisioning

In chapter 2, we discussed the importance of vision as one of the foundational elements of brand character. A good vision is relatively simple to build – but it is definitely not easy! It takes effort and dogged determination to build and deliver a vision that involves and engages staff. Our preferred model for articulating vision is taken from James Collins and Jerry Porras in their 1996 article entitled 'Building Your Company's Vision'. This model of vision is less about writing vision and mission 'statements' and more about defining core ideology and an envisioned future. However, we do not believe they went far enough, and so have expanded their model to create a much more holistic base on which to build a brand strategy.

Core ideology consists of two elements – values and purpose. Values are the foundational elements of vision and it pays to develop them with care. Many organisations will have a set of values that they believe exist within the company. Often though, individuals within the organisation would struggle to verbalise those values. The reason for this is that values are often implied. They may be inherited from business owners, or even the original founder.

The challenge in building a vision that can be embraced by the whole organisation is that it works best when staff have been involved in its development. This can be a big step for the business leader – but in our experience, is well worth the risk. It's all about getting buy-in

[1] *Collins, J. & Porras, J. (1996) Building Your Company's Vision – Harvard Business Review, Vol. 74, Iss. 5, pp65-77*

to the process and where staff see that their opinion is both sought and valued, they will invariably connect with the process. So values should be re-articulated with the help of staff. This can be done in a workshop environment and with careful facilitation a maximum of 5 or 6 core values can be identified. It is important when doing this to describe the words and articulate their meaning in the context of the organisation i.e. what they mean to you.

The purpose of the organisation is the next step to developing core ideology. Defining purpose is in some ways a replacement for the more traditional 'mission statement'. But where many mission statements are aspirational descriptions of what an organisation would like to do, a purpose is much more a statement of what it is here to do, a raison d'être for the business. So define the purpose with care – and above all be sure that you are articulating the real purpose of the business and not the outcomes. What's the difference? It may be tempting to say that your purpose is 'to make money' but that is not a purpose, rather it is an outcome of effectively delivering on the real purpose. So a better purpose statement may be 'to provide a safe and secure environment for the benefit of those who might visit, work or live in the area.'[2]

Next we look at the envisioned future of the business. In this model, we are looking to identify one 'Big Hairy Audacious Goal' or BHAG! A BHAG is a long-term goal – typically between 20 and 30 years ahead – that is aspirational, very hairy and very audacious. Be bold about setting long-term goals. Big goals inspire buy-in and encourage high performance. By setting goals that are far into the future, you effectively remove current personality and skill-set from the ultimate achievement of the goal. The difference between a short-term goal and a big hairy long-term one is that with the short-term goal, the mind will apply constraints around current achievability. It's hard to set a goal one, two or even three years ahead that you don't believe that you have the current capability of achieving. The beauty of the long-term goal is that current skill-sets are less of an issue. Having set the long-term goal, you can set shorter term goals that can be quantified as taking you in the direction of the BHAG but that you can achieve within the given timescale.

Having set the big goal, describe what it looks like. Allow your people to daydream and imagine what things look like when the goal has been achieved. What do the clients look like? How many staff are there in the business – are you in the same location? How are you perceived in the community? What is your reputation? What is your turnover? By describing yourself in the future, your people begin to visualise the future and their position in it. This is an incredibly powerful way of moving the aspiration to a vision of the future that is exciting, invigorating, challenging and inspiring.

With the values, purpose and direction of the company set, it is important to ground the envisioned future back to the day to day activities of the business. This is achieved by developing a 'how' statement. This statement says, in very general terms, how the organisation can go about delivering in the context of the vision. This statement should be simple and as short as possible. As an example, when Starbucks undertook this exercise, their 'how' statement was 'one cup at a time'. This simple but powerful statement encompasses all they do. It talks about the importance of each customer, about quality and about consistent delivery. Most importantly though, it deals with the everyday operation of Starbucks in a way that the more nebulous and ethereal values and purpose statements cannot. The 'how' statement is a way of grounding the envisioned future firmly in the here and now.

Building culture

The 'how' statement of the vision is very powerful, but on its own is not enough to move vision towards culture. Culture is where delivery happens — it's the powerhouse of great quality and customer service. An envisioned culture empowers the team to deliver first time and every time. To extend vision into culture requires two things — principles and behaviours.

Principles are the things that, as a business, you won't do. They are your 'lines in the sand'. It can be argued that principles are implied from values. For example, a value that many business share is integrity. Many things can be implied by the use of the word integrity — maybe you mean that you will pay your bills on time or that you won't overcharge your clients. The difficulty is that the things implied may not be where the focus was intended. Articulated principles allow you to focus your primary meaning from individual values. NRG Business networks[3], for example, operate just two principles — 'we won't lie' and 'we won't just do it for the money'. By articulating the principles that are most important to them, they begin to build a framework into which all business operations can be fitted. Make your principles specific and memorable and your people will be more likely to operate within them.

culture is where **delivery** happens

Setting behaviours further completes the day to day framework of normal activity and allows staff and board alike to behave towards each other, their clients and other stakeholders in ways that strengthen brand promises. In the end, it's behaviours that form the basis of

experience. And as we have said, experience is what drives retention
– both internally and externally. A clearly articulated, attainable and
agreed set of behaviours is the cornerstone to creating a brand culture
that delivers consistent experience. Don't be tempted to skim over this
part of the process. This area is the key to your brand success. Spend
time with your people defining and agreeing behaviours that can be
applied across all of the business interfaces. These are the 'we will'
statements of your business – 'we will treat everyone with respect',
'we will be reliable', 'we will deliver on time, every time' are just some
examples of powerful behaviour statements. Ensure that they are both
accessible and achievable and you will begin to create a culture of
success in which your brand can flourish.

Defining the landscape

The landscape in which your business operates is one that includes
customers, staff, competitors and suppliers. Each group has its own
unique characteristics which need to be researched and understood.
Do you have a picture of your ideal customer? Do you know what
his or her needs are or do you rely on assumptions made a long time
ago. Do you know what is going on in their world? How often do
you research their market trends and challenges? These are important
questions that apply across the board.

When defining the landscape, there is no substitute for hard work.
Define the research as a task and schedule it in with existing work.
This is not a time for skimping on detail. It is imperative that your data
about competitors and customers is up-to-date and accurate. So what
data do you need?

Customers:

- Industry trends — take an interest in your customers' industries — what's going on in their world.
- Latest company results — be aware of your customers' successes and failures — you may be able to help!
- Personnel changes — key staff changes can have an impact on your relationships. These may not be problematic, but any changes will create transitions that need to be managed.
- Strategic directional changes — don't be caught napping when your customer announces to the world that they are changing direction completely.
- Latest product offerings — keep abreast of your customers' R&D and new products.
- Competitor analysis — it pays to understand the nature of your customers' competitors. Once you do you will have a clearer insight into their issues and be in a better position to add value.

Competitors:

- Product — know your competitors' product sets — you will need to demonstrate your ability to perform better.
- Structure — how do their structures offer them advantage or hinder their advance?
- Pricing — you should not try to compete on price alone, but it pays to be aware of your competitors' pricing strategies.
- Successes and failures — learn from both, other peoples mistakes and triumphs can be a source of insight.
- Competitor trends — as far as possible, you should be leading the trends, but where you aren't, don't get left out in the cold as the marketplace changes.

Whilst it is important to understand the competitive landscape that you inhabit, it is also wise to define ideals for both staff members and suppliers. Spend some time with your HR team to define the 'must haves' for new staff appointments. When building a managed culture, attitude is definitely a precursor to aptitude. A prospective employee with a fantastic attitude can be trained to overcome shortcomings in skill-set. The reverse is much harder. So when defining the ideal employee, set a base line skill level, but then concentrate on attitudes. A good question to ask when employing someone is: 'will this person strengthen or damage the brand?' – get it right and you will build a strong effective team. Get it wrong and you will have an expensive and messy problem down the road.

The same applies to suppliers – take time to define acceptance criteria for accepting new suppliers. Not least of these criteria should be whether a supplier's values and ethics will devalue yours. Part of your 'image' with stakeholders is derived from the company you keep. If you get a name for dealing with disreputable suppliers, you will inevitably be tarred with the same brush. The power of association is very strong, so choose the people that you do business with carefully.

Brand plan

The brand plan will address the who, what, when and where questions. In order to move the business forward and to start on the journey from where you are now to the envisioned future, you need to have a plan. Let's take a look at what is involved in the brand plan.

Who

This is about defining resources and building a staff profile for the company. Start with an organisational chart and replace names with roles. This will allow you to see at a glance what the spread of skills is across the organisation — albeit at a high level. To accompany this, it is a useful exercise to build a skills matrix which will allow you to see what skills you have present in the organisation. This information begins to paint a picture or snapshot of the business as it stands now in relation to people and skills.

From this exercise you can begin to build a capacity plan which maps roles and skills with projected growth and allows you to see where and when new people or skills need to be added to the organisation. With a strong capacity plan in place, the business can forecast cash flow and profitability as it grows both in terms of turnover and staff and also manage that growth not just react to it as it happens.

ask yourself this question — 'is this **working** for the business?'

This is also an excellent time to revisit the organisation chart in terms of responsibilities and accountabilities. It's not our place to tell you how you should organise your business in terms of hierarchy and reporting structures — you know best what works in your environment. We would ask you to consider what you have and question its validity though. Is your structure a spin-off from a bygone age or the way you think it 'should be done'? If you answered yes to either of these questions, then maybe it's time to take a good look at your structure and ask yourself the question — 'is this working for the business?' The key thing is that once a structure is in place it should be communicated and understood throughout the organisation. Be very clear about who is responsible for what (especially in the leadership team) and then stick to it. Make your people accountable and they will make themselves accountable. It's a virtuous circle.

What

Can all of your people describe your product set? In this section of the brand strategy, we describe the products, their features and benefits and how they relate to each other. You may be surprised – especially in the service sector – how few businesses have a well articulated product definition outside of brochures or other marketing collateral. Is familiarisation a part of staff induction for example? Take this opportunity to write down just what your product set is (and don't forget to keep it up-to-date as your products evolve and change). As part of this exercise, it may be helpful to articulate the kind of problems that your product or service can solve for your clients. This will have the knock-on effect of enabling your staff to recognise potential clients when they see them.

Price is always a key question that is agonised over and hotly debated. Having done the work to define and understand the landscape from both the client and competitor viewpoints, you will have an idea of market averages for your products. The question now becomes – is your brand strong enough to be able to lift the business away from the strictly price-based competition model? Are your customers prepared to pay a premium for working with you or do they only care about price? The weighting that is associated with price will vary from sector to sector with some industries being more heavily biased towards price. Setting a price that reflects the value that clients derive from the relationship that they have with the brand ensures that brand equity is constantly improved.

As well as understanding, defining and managing your product set, this is the time to set out your service delivery package. The way that you deliver your product or service is as important as the product itself. A quality product whose delivery and aftercare disappoint will have only limited success. Market position is intrinsically linked to the position you hold in the minds of your stakeholders. Your 'mind-set' position is created and nurtured through the effective delivery of service that matches your clients expectation. It follows, therefore, that a planned and managed service delivery framework is vital to any well written strategy.

Finally, don't be afraid to set targets and goals around your product set. Plan the growth of each element. Take time to understand which parts of your portfolio are the most profitable and which deliver the best customer retention ratios. Be hard-nosed and, where necessary, be ruthless. If a part of your product set is neither profitable nor holds a high value for your customers, do something about it. That something may be to overhaul the product so that it becomes more profitable or it may be that you cut it completely. Plan growth now. To leave it all to chance may be exciting, but the risk of failure is high. Plan business growth, plan capacity growth and plan product development activities.

When

All planning activity involves a time-line, a start point, an end point and a list of activities that join the two. Planning for growth means that you will inevitably need to know when things are to happen because a large part of the ongoing implementation of strategy is to monitor progress towards the planned targets and goals. If you don't have a project management skill-set, now is the time to go and get one! Get some training, employ someone, ask your existing staff − it's up to you. Most organisations are fairly complex and will have unique planning challenges. Understanding how issues of resource availability, risk and dependency can scupper your plans, will allow you to build contingency that dramatically increases the chance of delivering on those plans.

A key element of planning is to recognise and monitor the marker points on the journey. These markers are the key events that are identified as being critical to the success of any venture. When do certain things need to have happened by in order to say that the plan is progressing successfully? Markers could be the points where targets are hit, for example, in turnover or number of new clients. They could also mark significant events such as the launch of a new product or moving in to a new office. These markers are used firstly to decide when these things should happen and secondly to measure progress as activity happens. They will often be reporting points where people with particular responsibilities can relay progress to the board.

When the timeline has been established and you know where the marker points are along the way, a last consideration is dependency. Identify which tasks are dependent upon other tasks completing successfully. When you know where these intersections and dependencies lie, you will also be able to identify the risks that you have built in to the plan.

Risk in any complex plan is inevitable. Tasks influence each other and outside influences need to be considered. It's not risk in itself that makes a plan more or less likely to succeed though – it's the management, or lack of management, of those risks that will be the deciding factor. Mitigation of risk will often result in contingency planning – managing the 'what ifs' is an essential part of strategic planning. A side benefit is that any plan that has carefully considered risk, and mitigated for it, will help to manage expectation at a sustainable level. This happens because confidence is based on the ability to deliver through risk and not by spending too much time replanning because of unforeseen issues.

however

beautiful

the strategy

you should occasionally look at the results

Winston Churchill

Where

Careful positioning of products and services within a defined marketplace can make the difference between success and failure in the implementation of the holistic brand strategy. Positioning is about identifying sales channels, distribution channels and communication channels which support the brand proposition. Now is the time to define your channels. What channels will you use to sell your products? Online, cold calling, consultative sales, networking and referral selling are all valid choices, and there are many more when we start to consider combinations of methods. There is no right or wrong method as long as it is right for you, fits within your brand values and ensures that you don't oversell your product or service.

it's about

three

things

Where do you educate your audience about your product or service? If you use advertising, can you identify which adverts are successful? How much do you need to educate your audience to the benefits of your product set? The opportunities for entering into a dialogue with your target market are increasing almost daily – blogging, online networking (both business and social) – viral campaigns, the list goes on.

The key thing is that you are in a dialogue. Gone are the days when you can talk at your customers and tell them what they think. We live in an age of ever-increasing sophistication and a failure to engage our audiences now will devalue the brand down the road. This is the age of the conversation – our communication is as much about audience response as it is about our ideas. To build a strong brand involves a process of guiding and managing those conversations to deliver not just information, but brand experience.

Alongside all of this planning, regular review points should be identified and dropped into the plan. As Sir Winston Churchill once said, 'however beautiful the strategy, you should occasionally look at the results.' With the best will in the world, things change, things don't always happen the way that you expected and the big wide world is always on hand to toss a spanner or two into your beautiful strategy. It is the responsibility of the owners of the brand strategy to regularly monitor, and where necessary adjust, the strategy so that it not only adds value at the point of inception, but that it continues to add value throughout its life. The brand plan is a living thing − it should be a working document not left to gather dust in a filing system or bookcase.

Brand delivery

The final part of the strategy is concentrated on delivery. Here we talk about how to build a framework in which delivery can take place. In later chapters we will talk about keeping the brand strategy going on a day-to-day basis. This is about defining processes and procedures, managing quality issues and building an architecture that builds consistency into activity across the business. In short, brand delivery is about three things: Do it now, do it well and do it again. The emphasis in delivery is doing it − not action for action's sake, but concerted, consistent and regular actions that build credibility with all of your stakeholders and ultimately build brand.

Do it now

The process that we describe in chapter 7 lays out a simple brand diagnostic that you can undertake to assess the state of your brand as it stands now. An outcome of the diagnostic will be that you will find areas of your business that require immediate action. That action may be remedial or preventative but it must be started as quickly as possible. The negative impact of identifying issues and doing nothing can be considerable. The single most demotivating internal behaviour in businesses is that of a leadership team that talks but doesn't act. The imperative therefore is to ensure action, but beware of knee-jerk reaction, the two are not the same. Any action should be timely but considered and always leading towards delivery of the brand strategy.

Staff buy-in is a major factor of the implementation of any brand strategy and the surest way of achieving staff buy-in is by building momentum. Momentum is a continuous movement in one direction and is reliant on the input of energy to keep it going. So consistent, continual input is required to maintain brand momentum. What small, frequent activities could you build in to your business to help to build brand momentum?

An action that can be taken immediately is a review of processes. Many businesses fail to reach their potential in terms of margins and profitability because they have inefficient or inappropriate processes in place – or worse still, none at all. Each business is different and we would not advocate a one size fits all approach to building business process. What is important is that processes are designed with two things in mind. Firstly, staff are empowered to deliver the experience that the brand promises. Secondly, they can do it in an efficient way that ensures productivity, and thus profitability, is enhanced.

A key element to build process, ensure staff buy-in and increase momentum is the ability to say with confidence what is working and what is not. The only way to achieve that confidence is by ensuring the metrics[4] you use are appropriate and reliable. Collecting data about day-to-day activity is an intrinsic part of brand delivery. A note of caution however; metrics are not the be-all and end-all. Remember the old saying 'you can't fatten a pig by weighing it'.

[4]   *By metrics we mean measurements and analysis*

YOU CAN'T FATTEN A PIG BY WEIGHING IT

Don't allow the metrics to take over — they are a tool for measuring progress, no more. The trick here is to have the smallest number of metrics possible that will give you focused, reliable data that can be extrapolated easily to provide the confidence needed.

Do it well

Quality is everything. Your customers don't look on quality as a benefit or a feature, they look on it as a given. This is not a differentiator for businesses, it's a minimum requirement. Don't think that you can get away with 'buy from us — we have a high quality product'. Who would buy your product or service if it wasn't high quality? Build in a level of quality that is appropriate for your marketplace and make sure that you always achieve or exceed the quality level.

Quality control is an important part of ensuring that quality standards are being met throughout the business — both in the product itself and in every aspect of its delivery and aftercare. Review your quality checking procedures if you have them and if not, build some. Do they give you reliable data that enables you to be confident in the quality of your product and service delivery? If they don't, do something about it now. Quality is a huge factor in customer satisfaction. It is also a huge factor in job satisfaction for your staff. Can they be proud of the product they are selling, marketing and delivering? If it's appropriate for your business type, do you need to consider ISO certification as a means of quality assurance? These are questions only you can answer.

The delivery of quality has the effect of creating a match between promise and experience. Your key task as a brand is the delivery of consistent experience and your quality standards go a long way towards that delivery. Match promise and action and you build positive perception. Positive perception leads to trust and trust is what keeps your customers coming back. Define the quality standards across the business, build the processes that support its delivery and measure performance.

Do it again

Repeatability is an essential for the ongoing delivery of a holistic brand. The delivery of experience at every point of contact — every time means that steps must be taken to ensure that excellence can be replicated time and again. Consistency doesn't happen by accident, it must be planned and managed. Consistency alone is not enough — after all, you can be consistently bad! Creating a service which delivers great experience every time is the goal.

We have said over and over that retention is a major key to building a strong brand — both customer and staff. The ability to consistently repeat success is a key to that retention. For customers it brings the quality expectation that the mass-produced age has bought (even in the bespoke market). In the same way that your clients expect their cornflakes will taste the same every morning, they expect the delivery of your service to consistently add value. They disconnect with your brand when that delivery leaves them feeling that something has changed and they are not sure that they like it.

Staff retention has a direct correlation to staff success. When your staff are empowered to succeed, they will succeed and success is a very powerful motivator. For many people, the perception of their own success can be a strong driver for their career. Smart businesses build an environment that has the right mix of culture, motivation and processes to create success. How do people achieve success? By being able to do their job well and by understanding a direct link between their contribution, customer satisfaction and business success.

Your strategy, therefore, must include processes and methods for ensuring the delivery of repeatable excellence. Build it, deliver it, measure it, monitor it and as our friends from Nike like to say, 'just do it'. Do it now, do it well and do it again.

With a brand defined and a strategy in place, it only remains to implement it. You know the direction in which you are headed, the values you hold and your core purpose. You have built the plan that tells you how and when you are going to achieve your goals and you have the processes in place to deliver consistent excellence time and again. So far, so good, but now it's time to get on with it, and for that you need two things — and they're both buy-in. In the next chapter we will look at how that buy-in is achieved.

Chapter 4

Getting buy-in

The successful implementation of holistic brand strategy is dependant on two things. Those two things are buy-in from the leadership team and buy-in from staff. Both are of equal importance and one without the other will result in frustration. Building a holistic brand is extremely hard work, particularly at the beginning of the process. To undertake this task without the complete co-operation of the leadership team and without a high level of buy-in from staff, will make it an uphill struggle.

The first challenge is to get your leadership team on board with the process. This is a step that cannot be skipped. Holistic branding is essentially a top-down process, meaning that the leaders in the organisation must drive change. Driving change through an organisation is a tricky business that is not about issuing autocratic edicts, but is the result of passion, communication, delivery and consistency. These are attributes of a bought-in leadership, not of a management structure that is merely cascading (and inevitably diluting) corporate will.

There are several ways of gaining buy-in from the leadership team, but the start point is to encourage your people to understand the benefits involved. Have a look at the A to Z of benefits in appendix 3. This is a varied list that covers most areas of the business. You can add your own, of course, but the benefits broadly fit in to three categories – financial, cultural and communicational.

The financial benefits are threefold. The first is increased turnover resulting from a strategically aligned marketing function. This is the kind of marketing that consistently delivers new business in a managed way, helping to smooth out the peaks and troughs of the

THE DIFFERENCE BETWEEN

INVOLVEMENT

&

COMMITMENT

IS LIKE HAM AND EGGS...

purely tactical approach. The second is an increase in profitability that stems from improved productivity and reduced overheads as a result of managed recruitment, development and performance. The third financial benefit is in the area of brand equity. A strong brand, supported by a well managed strategy and delivered holistically, will consolidate the value of the business and enhance both succession planning and exit strategy.

The cultural benefits are a more motivated, and thus more productive, workforce, greater clarity of direction as a result of managed internal communication policies, and a greatly improved team dynamic. Organisational culture, as we have said before, is enormously important. Well defined, positive culture will release energy and enthusiasm that drives performance improvement. An understanding of the core ideology of the business and its envisioned future, allied to behaviours that ground those fundamentals into everyday life, are the power source of the performing business. Leading this kind of company is so much easier and more rewarding than one fuelled by negativity, inefficiency and consistent underperformance.

Communicational benefits arise because holistic branding encourages the creation of an aligned message generation engine that delivers well articulated, relevant and clear messages. The results derived from this type of messaging are firstly more effective marketing communications and secondly a more transparent internal communication process. The ability to include a clear, consistent and strategically driven message set in marketing activity generates brand recognition and trust — even in the most cutting edge tactical delivery. That same clear, consistent and strategically driven message set, used as part of the internal communication process, goes a very long way to building trust and clarity amongst staff.

THE CHICKEN IS

INVLVED

THE PIG IS

COMMITTED

Martina Navratilova

So management buy-in is gained because of two things; the belief that the process will deliver fundamental business improvement, and the realisation that the delivery of improved organisational performance will make the task of leadership more focused and enjoyable.

The second area of buy-in is from staff. It's difficult to overstate the importance of commitment to the process from staff. Without it the process is all but doomed. In the end, it will be the people at the coalface that deliver the implementation of your brand strategy, and that will happen best when your people are passionate about delivering the brand. There are any number of methods and tools for establishing staff buy-in, but they broadly cover two areas — communication and involvement.

Communication is paramount. Without effective and real communication in place it won't be long before your people feel as though they are in a mushroom farm — kept in the dark and fed on 'organic growing medium'! Lack of communication is a sure-fire way to develop a negative, low energy, cynical culture that will stop your change program in its tracks. If you want your people on board, you have to talk to them. Be upfront about the reasons for change. Talk through the brand strategy and leave plenty of space for people to question. When people question your strategy, what they are really doing is building their own understanding. Above all don't brush aside people's fears. Any change brings with it a fear of the unknown and a sense of insecurity that are very real.

By introducing structured and intentional staff involvement in the holistic branding process, buy-in can be achieved by ownership. When staff are involved in the decision making process, particularly in the area of brand planning and brand delivery, they begin to own the brand and its implementation. From a purely pragmatic point of view, all of us are more likely to be 'on board' with an idea, a new business process, or a new way of doing things if we were involved in its generation. So the challenge for the business leader who is trying to achieve buy-in for the holistic branding process is how to involve staff in the directional elements of the process.

What can help enormously is to have employee representation in the early stages of brand strategy development. So by having employees contributing to the articulation of values, purpose and direction, those employees will become 'champions' of the process as it is rolled out across the business. One way that makes that engagement even more valuable is to include at least one representative who is normally reticent about buying-in to organisational change – the team cynic if you like. When those people become your advocates across the business, change becomes a lot more likely to succeed quickly.

Don't worry, buy-in is possible – in fact, it's much easier than you might think. The trick is to ensure that it is achieved both at the leadership level and the staff level. It takes effort, but by consistently delivering meaningful communication, and by introducing genuine team involvement, you can take your people with you.

Chapter 5
Implementing the strategy

Implementing a brand strategy is analogous to building a dry stone wall, and you will find this analogy truly helpful. Imagine a well constructed dry stone wall. Now imagine leaning a large version of your company logo against the wall. Which better represents a brand — the wall or the logo? Obviously the logo is the visual attraction, and 90% of people will probably opt for the logo, but of course it's the wall that counts as we have already demonstrated.

Without the wall the logo falls over, and when we implement a brand strategy we're actually beginning to build a wall that won't fall over. But why a dry stone wall, not an ordinary brick wall? Well, dry stone walls are not bonded by an external agent (mortar) but are constructed so that every stone holds another one in place, and therefore every wall is different, as every business is. This 'natural bonding' is like a positive company culture which allows you to build a great brand — it has to hold together by a common understanding and buy-in from everyone. If a brand culture is imposed upon an existing organisation by the powers that be (mortar) it will be eroded if the brand means one thing to one person and something different to the next. These differences will be passed on to customers, and if their experience of the company is not consistent across all entry points, the brand reputation will be damaged and may eventually collapse.

Service, reliability, staff, policies, behaviours, vision and values are just some of the things which form the constituent parts of a brand. And just as the stones in the wall are all different, each of these elements of your business are different. The skill of the dry stone waller is in selecting the right stone for the right part of the wall and in building them together so that they form a single cohesive whole.

A well-built dry stone wall will last for generations. Why is this? Is it just because the structure itself is inherently strong? Well that's part of the reason, but just as importantly it's easy to fix damaged areas because the blocks are not artificially bonded together. It's also easy to move or adjust as the landscape changes. How long-lasting is your brand? How easy is it to fix worn or damaged parts?

Before we begin to discuss how to implement a brand strategy, it's a good idea to quickly cover how we got to this point in the process.

We began by explaining what a holistic brand is – how it is the combination of all internal organisational experiences and perceptions which build a company culture, and every external experience and perception that is built up around a business by customers and suppliers. We explained why it is experiences and perceptions that rule, rather than the commonly accepted view that it is primarily the visual look and marketing messages that create a brand.

In chapter 2 we went on to show you how to define your brand. We showed how the four elements of the brand wheel comprise character, personality, voice, and talents, and these are the basis on which we build a brand strategy. We showed how each of these areas cross-relate in all aspects of a business.

We then explored how to build a brand strategy through a model that begins with the brand manifesto, then continues with a brand plan, and is completed by brand delivery.

the concept
brand
is like

of holistic

ing

a

stone wall

In chapter 4 we discussed how important it is to get buy-in from all levels within the organisation before we begin to develop an internal culture or create a brand strategy. Buy-in is the primary agent that will begin to form the 'natural bonding' that generates the momentum to build a strong, positive internal culture. We showed that without the strength of a positive internal culture, then external experiences and perceptions will always be misaligned, mismanaged and miscommunicated.

Structured implementation is vital

However, once you have a strategy, have worked out the brand plan, and understood the methodology behind brand delivery, then what? Many consultants give advice on specific business topics, but often tend to leave with the impression that it is your responsibility whether or not you do anything with the advice! We believe that the implementation of the strategy is every bit as vital as the strategy itself. You can have created a great strategy, but without implementing it correctly, then you will simply undo all the hard work you have put in so far. A strategy has to be reinforced consistently across every area because perceptions and experiences have to align no matter what the opportunity or challenge, whether it is an internal issue or an external message.

But where to start?

Unless you and the other board members have bought into, and understand the concepts and reasons behind holistic branding, then you are going to find implementing the brand strategy very difficult. Martin Luther King said, 'I can see the promised land!', so you too have to see where this process can lead you to. As a leader, you have to envisage the future before anyone else can.

There is little or no point in producing a brand manifesto that encapsulates all the behaviours that you want to see displayed by everyone else in the organisation, if you yourself at board level do not remember what they are! Before you begin implementation, make sure you are passionate enough to see the brand behaviours worked out in your own life. It has to become as natural as breathing air. It has to be real. It has to be so ingrained in the board members that if you are asked what the behaviours are, then you can reel them off because they live in you. Holistic branding is not an 'imposed from without' regime – it is a 'lived out' lifestyle that everyone buys-in to. That process always starts at the top.

In this chapter we will address a range of implementation issues and explain the rationale (not a methodology, because every organisation is different) to implement everything we have built to this point. If you have taken these things on board so far, by now you have all the building blocks that can make your own brand much stronger. We will discuss the differences between tactical marketing and brand awareness, the effective use of web-based marketing, and how to measure response rates in differing media. We will also address knowledge management, authority levels, and differentiators (or USPs), and align all elements (such as the HR strategy through to the financial planning and other business plans you need to run a successful operation) so that we begin to develop a strong holistic brand.

buy-in

is the primary agent for natural bonding

Some of these topics will be self-evident to you, some of it may have previously been covered by consultants in one area or another, and some of it seen as the marketing people's mystique or the web developers remit, best left alone. To successfully implement your strategy, there has to be a co-ordinated effort by all internal departments and external agencies, so that each area begins to develop only in line with the strategy and not head off in different directions. Both internal sales/marketing departments and external advertising agencies are prime examples of this because they think visually and tactically. The 'wow' factor in visual work is vital, but unless it reinforces the overall strategy, looks part of the family, or continues to convey the brand ethos, then momentum will be lost.

Unless, of course, you are a completely new start-up enterprise, no organisation begins this process with a clean sheet of paper. There will be pre-existing prejudices, behaviours and attitudes held by staff members, and predetermined practices and processes that have all built the current level of experiences and expectations. There will be existing advertisements, brochures and web sites, some good, some not, some aligned, some not! All these will have formed a combination of both positive and negative perceptions about the organisation. Challenging and changing these perceptions can create a spiral effect where every right action and every positive response creates an upward lift. Implementation is a bit like snakes and ladders – the key is to avoid the snakes!

Someone has to be in control

This is fundamental to a strategic implementation of a brand strategy. Traditionally, brand has been viewed as a subset of the marketing department, but this normally makes tactical marketing more important than the brand strategy. As we have demonstrated, holistic branding is strategic, marketing is essentially tactical, and so control of brand strategy has to be raised above the interdepartmental level, and returned to board level. As there is not yet the training or qualifications towards a career in brand management in the holistic

sense within universities, there has to be a temporary situation whereby you can designate one director to have overall authority for the implementation of the brand strategy. Without this centralised authority, each department will continue in isolation, probably not checking with each other, or without checking their procedures and policies actually align with the brand strategy.

Put brand authority back in the boardroom! It is not only essential for internal issues, it is even more important that board level authority rules over external organisations who want to do what they think is best for your brand! External agencies persuading a manager is one thing, to persuade a whole board is entirely different!

The three areas of implementation

Once you have a brand strategy (the sum total of the brand manifesto, the brand plan, and the brand delivery) then you are in a solid position to begin implementing it. You will know that some of these issues can be addressed immediately, and that this is going to be an ongoing process, and that you will have to measure for effectiveness at all stages. If you have already achieved a level of buy-in through personnel participation in building the brand strategy, then a number of different issues can be implemented by different departments simultaneously. This is because they can now all refer back to the same brand strategy instead of acting independently in a silo situation. However, breaking implementation into three broad areas assists the overall implementation strategy, because the level of control that is held over different areas varies from company to company, and is affected by management ability and authority. These three basic areas are not hard-wired, but can be adapted according to the size and set up of your particular organisation. You will need to build your own diagram and place all activities into one area or another.

The core area contains all the elements that are purely internal aspects of the organisation such as culture, personnel issues, physical environment, financial, capacity and other business planning and internal processes. These are the things that you can control, adjust or rectify. As there are no fixed activities in any of these areas, you may want to include your products or services here, for example, if you do not rely heavily on external input such as materials, or primarily provide a service. The key is that you have complete authority within the organisation to see change instigated or implemented.

The second area covers those elements that have a crossover between the internal and the external — such as customer relations, sales, HR. These are areas where you are open to outside influences but instigate control primarily from within. For example, you may have an in-house marketing department that also relies on external agency input, or a sales force that is dependent on the actions of a wholesale chain. The overall control will still emanate from within the organisation, possibly via a departmental manager, but the control of the external agency is more difficult to manage. This crossover is the area which, if conquered and correctly managed in line with the brand strategy, will prove to be the most effective — it eventually controls the external messages and public face of the company.

Finally, there is the third area which relies heavily on external influences. This is where control is vitally important, because you have to ensure the work of external agencies is always referred back to the brand strategy to ensure alignment. This area covers advertising agencies, PR agencies, supply chains, delivery subcontractors, etc. For example, you may not have an in-house personnel department and therefore rely on recruitment agencies on the one hand, and a personnel consultant on the other. Many Franchise organisations lean heavily on the performance of the franchisees, and although elements of a franchise may be directly controlled through internal procedures and materials, they have to rely heavily on controlling the actions and behaviours of the franchisees to deliver the goods.

Although implementation of the brand strategy can be done simultaneously across the company, simply trying to fix the external area before tackling the internal area or the crossover area is putting the cart before the horse. This external area is probably most in need of improvement, but it cannot be continuously controlled unless the first two areas are running pretty smoothly. In all three areas, it has to be the board that assesses on a regular basis how the brand strategy is working, what is still weak, which areas have improved and which areas are really strong. Remember that metrics need to be constantly applied to every area of implementation on an ongoing basis. This way the brand strategy is constantly at the centre of every activity and progress then has tangible, time bound parameters.

Internal – directly under your control

Because these aspects of a business are entirely under your control it is the fundamental key to the other areas of implementation which may be more difficult to maintain in alignment with the brand strategy. Without tight control at this level, then you can never (or at least almost never) succeed in maintaining alignment of external messages, and when this happens, it's 'back to the stadium'!

Empower your personnel for change

The first part of the personnel issue is in dealing with the people you already have in the organisation. Your employees need to 'get the picture' of what the brand strategy is all about. People only do what people 'see'. If they can see it, they can embrace it, and when they embrace it, internal issues get solved and an aligned implementation is inevitable. But this is a slow, progressive process as you can't easily internal

under your control

crossover

partially or primarily
under your control

external

potentially outside
your
control

fire someone just because they are naturally negative or resistant to change! We have already dealt with getting buy-in in chapter 4. Suffice it to say here, that when you begin to develop a team who 'get the picture', they will become more positive, professional and focused on the brand, and you will have achieved your first objective. Additionally, your employment issues will drop dramatically, and this alone can save thousands on recruitment costs through high staff turnover. Essentially it will give you control over all the internal aspects of the business, align departments to the same goals, and provide the platform for external control.

Building the internal culture

Get this right and you are halfway there to controlling the other two areas of implementation, but it's a big ask whatever your staffing level is. The internal culture is the 'natural bonding' of the dry stone wall analogy we use. Just as we can picture the stones in the wall as different departments in an organisation fitting together, we can also visualise the stones in a more personal way. The stones are also 'living stones' – people built together to make the brand wall, held together by a common purpose, fitting together through a defined culture. We have already explained in chapter 3 the elements that make a brand manifesto, but we need to build on the theoretical and make it practical. Good communication is at the heart of culture because we all need to 'sing off the same hymn sheet' to build it.

There are several things you can instigate here to assist with bringing all personnel on board with the brand manifesto. Firstly, instigate a series of all-personnel meetings (or departmental meetings if the organisation is that large), so that the brand manifesto can be explained. If your company is small, it is even better to create a training day that is not just seen as a 'jolly', but sets the specific task of defining and creating a 'brand manifesto'. Because the company personnel created it, they will more readily take ownership of it.

Whichever way you develop the brand manifesto it will still have to be presented and re-presented to all personnel until all personnel 'get it' and begin to live it out every day.

Another method of instigating change is to introduce 'Plus Teams'. These are small teams that form to address a certain issue, and then disband, only for a new team to be formed to address another issue. They are called plus teams because their task is to recommend to the board ways of improving a specific issue that is currently seen as inefficient or negative, and change it from a minus aspect of the brand to plus point. Teams should be drawn from across the organisation, not just experts in one department, so that there are interdepartmental connections and so that everyone can feel involved at some point. This empowers everyone to feel they have a voice that is heard and a part to play in building the brand. It is, therefore, incumbent on the board to take up as many recommendations as are reasonable and affordable. Every recommendation that is rejected has to have a clearly valid reason or the power of the plus teams to influence change will be lost and the whole concept will rapidly turn negative.

Communication
One of the big areas that can hinder any brand is the level and quality of internal communication. This is well recognised, but also so often overlooked. A good brand manifesto will have built in recognition that good communication will be part of the brand. Building on this requires the board to be the prime movers, because personnel will be resistant to making comments for fear of reprisals. The culture needs to reflect that any comments that can positively improve the brand will be taken seriously. Without great communication channels the brand messages will be mixed when they reach the outside world, so it is worth investing time and effort in getting the internal messages and communication methodology working at peak performance. Again, use the plus teams!

Encouragement

We live in a world that is extremely negative, where good news doesn't seem to figure on the news channels very often. Mostly we see natural disasters, rumours of recession, wars and genocide, famines and pestilences, death and destruction. We imbibe this negativity almost without thinking — it's the world we live in. So it is not surprising that many companies have worried people participating in, and unintentionally building, a negative working atmosphere. What is surprising is that encouragement is so low on company agendas. Encouragement costs nothing and yet can be so culture changing and uplifting. Give a cheerful word, an encouraging smile, and cards to say 'thanks' for something (not just for a job well done) on a regular basis — all these are basics in building positivity.

Reward and recognition is always valuable. If you are not a leader that easily empowers others or likes to reward their success, then you need to change. The commitment and improvements shown by staff need to be appreciated visibly and verbally on a regular basis if you are serious about building a strategic implementation. Momentum is a force that builds on a smooth curve. It has to be built step-by-step, day in, day out, not inconsistently or stop-start. Remember the spiral effect that every right action creates a lift in positivity, in experience and finally in external perception. Reward and recognition is a vital part of gaining that momentum.

Assess the recruitment policy

As we have said, you will already have existing staff, so before you take on anyone else, begin to implement a recruitment policy based on the brand strategy. Recruit according to your brand rather than simply fill a job role specification. Almost no one does this, and yet it is so important, as all new personnel affect the culture. The policy can be developed with your HR Manager, if you have one, or discussed at board level and then communicated to external recruitment agencies.

The first step is to create an 'ideal candidate' profile (attitudinal, not job role), so you have the basis on which to select recruits for brand 'fit' every time, regardless of the job role. For example, you may want people who are self-motivated, teachable, team players, positive...

Obviously it will be much more expansive than this, so try to build a vivid word picture of the sort of attributes you want all new people to exhibit, remembering that you don't want clones of yourself or the personnel manager! Like-minded people are attracted, opposites tend to repel, and positive attitudes generate more positive attitudes. Having an overriding brand 'person profile' in writing before approaching a recruitment agency or placing recruitment advertisements, ensures not only generating the right calibre candidates, but also assists in dealing even-handedly with all candidates interviewed. Psychometric testing could be done online through a specialist organisation for the top two or three candidates, and this will strengthen the final choice with a rationale rather than emotion. This way you will form the basis for a better recruitment policy, know more accurately the personality you are taking on, and where their strengths and weaknesses lie. The ongoing training can be better tailored to suit the individual and will bring improvements across the organisation and the culture.

The 'Investors in People' award aids systematic training and empowerment at all levels, and can be an important tool in proving to your personnel that the organisation is seriously interested in their training and development within the context of the brand strategy. If they have bought into the brand strategy, then they will want training that makes the brand more effective, rather than request training that will simply enhance their next job move.

Personnel induction
The final issue that needs to be kept in mind is that every change in personnel will affect the brand, and this can happen at any time,

however far you have progressed in implementing the brand strategy. Most companies now have some sort of induction procedure for new staff members, but the importance of introducing new personnel to the brand culture is rarely recognised or included, however structured the process is. It seems self-evident that an induction into the brand principles, the behaviours required, and culture that pervades the working environment should be part of the induction process, because if it is not, then how do new people buy in?

In fact this is one of the biggest areas of potential downfall for a brand, because new personnel need to be integrated correctly to maintain the unity of the brand direction. Unresolved personnel issues are always the catalyst for disintegration. New staff cannot automatically become an integrated member of the brand culture until they understand it, and the culture can be damaged so easily without constant care and attention. We have witnessed one strong brand who took on additional and replacement personnel without helping them understand the brand, or introducing them to the dynamic of internal culture. The consequences were horrific. The brand suffered as the departments went in new and diverging directions, the brand messages no longer reflected the internal culture, and the net result was a mess. Someone had to pick up the pieces and repair the brand. This issue was expensive, and time-consuming to repair, resulting in a loss of brand momentum and credibility!

Planning and processes

Once you have a brand strategy, it is much easier to look at business planning in the context of where you want to go. For example, it assists capacity planning because you know which departments you need to strengthen and grow, and which ones will fall by the wayside. Implementing all your financial planning and internal production processes based on the brand strategy will pinpoint savings and cut duplication in procedures. It will also take into consideration the reduction in costs (such as recruitment) and ring-fence finance for growth areas that fit your direction.

It cannot be stressed too strongly that each internal area has to be assessed against its current position and alignment to the new brand strategy. Then, according to the need for realignment, deal with each department in turn. Working together, put policies and processes in place to ensure that internal working, interdepartmental communication and external contacts are all covered.

Many internal processes have an impact on delivery of the product or service you supply. Weak or unaligned processes can directly or indirectly affect the experiences and perceptions of the customer. Many of the marketing messages will rely also on the processes being robust enough to deliver, so processes and procedures are a prime area to be subjected to plus team scrutiny. It's a great methodology to reduce time delays and duplication, improve communication, involve people at all levels and bolster staff morale.

Physical environment
Alongside the personnel issues, it is beneficial to look at the physical working environment as one of the first areas for improvement, because alterations to the visual aspects of the working environment signal an intention to see the changes through on an ongoing basis. Visual reminders are a great way of reinforcing the core values, purpose and vision. A plus team can be set in place to investigate this area immediately following the initial brand meetings. Don't wait, even if you believe there will have to be other visual realignments in terms of corporate style to reflect 'the new you'. In fact, the corporate style is not one of the first things that should necessarily

change. Corporate style and messages can evolve and emerge in line with the new brand strategy, but getting the core behaviours and principles into the forefront of organisational thinking needs to be implemented upfront and is best facilitated by visual changes to the working environment. Changing the external visual strategy first will simply push organisational thinking back down the route of 'we've rebranded' when, of course, all you've done is change a visual identity, nothing more. Improving the physical working environment will change personnel perceptions for the better.

Crossover – partially or primarily under your control

This area covers those elements where you can reasonably expect to be in control, but may not be in total control at the current time. However, you have to ensure that your internal departments are all aligned, so that when they come into contact with the outside world, the brand messages are strong and clear, the brand values understood and core principles are adhered to. Depending on the size of your organisation, you will have one or more departments or several individuals that come into contact with external suppliers, customers, local media and the like. The crossover point is how well the brand is represented by these individuals. If you rely simply on their integrity, but have no measure of their level of integrity, then you have hit a danger point where the brand could be misrepresented, however innocently the actions or responses may be.

It is said of football, that the team that controls the midfield, controls the game, and the tactical decisions on when to utilise a 4-4-2 or 3-5-2 formation is the making or breaking of many a Premiership coach. So it is with implementation. If you control your 'midfield', the area of crossover between internal and external, you will eventually control the external perceptions and experiences. The result? A strong holistic brand that beats your competitors at their own game.

THE

TEAM THAT TAKES

CONTROL OF

THE MIDFIELD

DOMINATES

THE GAME

The work you do to build a positive internal culture, to bring clarity to your internal communications, and to put policies and processes in place that all align to the brand strategy, will pay dividends when it comes to those departments or personnel that interact with the outside world. The better they understand the brand manifesto with its values, principles and behaviours, then the less chance there is that they will act against those principles.

The sales function

Let's assume you have an internal sales department with a sales manager and several sales people on the road. Sales people can be notoriously loose cannons, because their sole focus is making a sale and gaining commission. Here is a danger point. Will they represent your brand only in such a way as to benefit the brand, or will they bend the rules to gain the sale? This is where a recruitment policy, based on brand 'fit', substantially alleviates these concerns. Implementing a policy that emphasises the brand values will be much stronger if you already know the integrity of the individuals – because you tested for it before employing them.

However, 'bending the rules' can also affect the consistent experiences and the subsequent perceptions of the customers in a positive way, but only if the solution does not conflict with the brand ethos. Where the issue is to resolve a customer's problem by thinking outside the box, then the result will be a positive experience, not a negative one, and becomes a plus in the mind of the customer for the next sale.

The accounting function

It isn't just customer-facing personnel that are involved with this crossover area. Your accounts personnel will deal with suppliers as well as customers. How good are your response times? Do you always pay on time, or do you tell 'porkies' to delay payments to your advantage? How good are your systems? Would you be concerned if the VAT man turned up on your doorstep? All these issues of integrity can affect perceptions for good or bad. How frustrated are you when no one picks up the phone, calls you back, or responds to voicemail messages or emails? Your accounts function not only keeps the finances in order, they affect customer and supplier perceptions with every phone call.

All these internal/external functions can be aligned and managed correctly if viewed and regulated against the bigger picture of a brand manifesto. The issue is often that these functions operate within a silo system — each separate from the other. Get cross-referencing in place through plus teams to assess procedures.

Pricing strategy
Although you may not be able to influence pricing as much as you would like at this moment in time, a pricing strategy can be developed to be in line with the progress you make while building a strongly recognisable brand. This is in the crossover area because many companies rely on outside suppliers or materials that influence the base costs. On the other hand, there is the balance of what the market will take and the current standing of the company.

Use this diagram to put an X on the line where you think you are now. Then place another X where you want to be in the future as aligned with your vision.

Cheapest   Most
expensive

Next, put an X on this diagram where you are now, and another X where you want to be. Here you have to balance whether or not you are seen as value-for-money (as opposed to cheap), and whether the benefits inherent in the company (such as reliability, service, etc.) outweigh the features of the product.

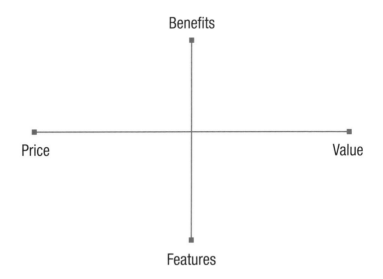

These two exercises will assist in aligning your pricing strategy with your vision. You can then begin to adjust prices towards where you want to be placed, as the organisation begins to align to the brand strategy. This methodology will show you too, that the way it is now, doesn't have to be the way it can be. Don't be controlled by price due to external circumstances and perceptions of the company – control the perceptions so you can control the pricing!

Public Relations and knowledge management

A Public Relations (PR) communication is no longer the animal it was – a simple press release sent out in the hope that a journal would find it interesting. It has changed to include writing your own product articles, creating blogs for others to read, getting that information in front of editors who get hundreds of articles every day for consideration – and they just do not want more of the same. A press release that says you've won another contract often isn't going to get much coverage – think how many companies will want to say they've got a contract for the 2012 Olympics!

Nowadays PR is better when it provides Editors with the authority and knowledge articles they are always on the lookout for. Good informational articles can be really effective, and is a great way to protect knowledge management. It is far better for a brand to disseminate the information it wishes, than allow misinformation through poor handling of the press.

If you are a larger organisation it is seriously worth investing in training for personnel who may interact with the press, not only through journalist interviews, but also for TV and radio interviews. This is an area where one wrong word can get a lot of coverage if taken out of context. Small instances like that have done huge harm to otherwise successful brands. Remember Gerald Ratner's slip of the tongue about the jewellery products they sold. One small statement for Gerald Ratner – one huge leap in customer perception! The repercussions were irreversible!

Customer relations
Many SME's have a CRM system of some sort. Keeping your data 'clean' and up-to-date is such an important factor when it comes to customer experiences. How many of us hate receiving mail when we have asked to be taken off a database, only to continue to get junk mail? Or mail that arrives for the attention of someone who left the organisation three years ago! It happens all the time in different ways, and it all boils down to bad lists or bad data cleansing.

Even worse, cancelling your membership of some sort, only to get an invitation to join the same organisation three weeks later! Nothing puts customers (and ex-customers) off faster!

This is a major area of crossover that goes wrong so very often and yet it is so simple to rectify with a brand strategy that includes a brand manifesto! Firstly, implement procedures now to check out your data cleansing, its frequency, and the procedures used. Train your personnel and make sure that different departments share vital data. This is where the silo system fails abysmally. One department holds one set of customer data, another holds a different set. They should marry, but they don't. Net result — unhappy customers, potentially bad blogs flying about and mismatching customer experiences!

keep your

data

'clean' and up-to-date

Much of your internal and crossover implementation will revolve around improving and aligning your procedures and training your personnel to think and live the brand manifesto. You need great communication skills, great teamwork, and great perseverance to make these issues fall into line, but although these issues could be a concern every time someone picks up the phone, sends an email or writes a letter (obviously these events happen every minute of the working day), there is no point becoming paranoid about it. The answer is to implement the brand manifesto in every way possible — educate personnel, supply training in customer relations where necessary, use plus teams. Implementing these actions ensures that all parts of the organisation understand what the guidelines are because the brand manifesto itself is built on trust. When brand behaviours live at the heart of the organisation you will have little cause for concern. This is one of the biggest benefits of holistic branding because you create an organisation where everyone desires to do the right thing for the brand, because they know ultimately, it will be good for them!

External – potentially outside your control

This is the area of implementation with the greatest impact on customer experiences and perceptions, but also the area most vulnerable to influences that can escalate outside an organisation's control. The question is, are you going to control your destiny, or will you allow others to shape your future? If you take control of the crossover area of implementation, this area becomes a lot more manageable. You begin to control the messages that get disseminated from your organisation. You control customer experiences through consistently great customer care. You can deliver great products through aligned processes. And you can control outside organisations that work on your behalf such as PR and advertising agencies. This is where you control outside advertising and communications messages through clearly briefed projects, and assess the work in line with the brand style and stance. Additionally you, can assess Return on Investment (ROI).

It is where corporate identity, style, tone and voice combine holistically from all areas of the organisation. Let's look at some of the methods:

Internet

There are now many methods to communicate with your customers, and the fastest growing area is the web. Having a traditional 'brochure-ware' site is no longer sufficient. People gather information from the web to compare products, write blogs and share their information.

Ensuring your website can be found through a combination of search engine optimisation and search engine marketing is more important than ever. Tools such as Google Adwords can be used, but be aware of the cost of 'click-through rates'. Used correctly it can be beneficial, but other cheaper options, such as continually updating the site with new information, researching and using the current keywords that people use to search for the items they need, can be very effective. Check out the Keyword Effectiveness Index (KEI) of your keywords.

There is no point in using the first keywords you think of in relation to your brand if millions of others use the same word. You probably wouldn't make the first one hundred pages on Google – and unless you can get to page one or two, then there's little chance of getting noticed! If you use a web agency, get them to use the appropriate keyword tracking software to refine the keywords they use.

This is just as true for B2B as it is for B2C companies. Which search terms represent your brand? Which words attract customers to your site? Work in conjunction with a good web team, but insist the messages you allow out are yours, not theirs. This can also be accomplished through the inclusion of a Content Management System (CMS) function on the site that allows your internal staff to upload certain areas of information instead of having to wait for the web agency to do it. It saves cost and allows up-to-the-minute information to be displayed as well!

Build appropriate and relevant links from other sites to yours. For example, if you are a member of a trade association see if you can get a mention on their site and a link to yours. Yell.com is worth considering in this respect.

Learn to assess the site statistics, or at least ask your agency to explain the difference between unique visits, where they were from, how long visitors stayed on site, and what the bounce rate is. All these will assist in building a clearer picture of how well the site is received, if it is doing its job (in addition to how good it looks), and whether it is corporate

Advertising
We have all heard the saying 'I know half my advertising works, but not which half!' Advertising per se is an expensive business, and only ever works if it is strategically targeted and is a continual drip feed.

One-off ad hoc adverts never work; they are just a waste of precious resources, so never let an eager advertising rep con you with 'I've got a spare page at half price....' Unless you book a campaign that is targeted to a specific audience and uses selected media, then save your money — there are other ways. If you do use advertising, then ensure response rates are measured by publication. This can be done with the inclusion of an identifier (for example, an ad in 'Boiler and Plumbing News' could be BPN1, BPN2, etc.). This way you will know the exact issue and publication from which a response form was obtained. If you rely on a contact phone line, ensure your operators always ask where they heard of the offer, etc.

There is also a distinct difference between tactical advertising (which requires tracking) and brand awareness advertising (which does not). Brand awareness is vital, particularly if you need to re-emphasise your brand and your distinctiveness, but as your brand becomes better known, so your awareness can be reduced even to a use of colour, style or even just a sound. Think of Eddie Stobart lorries or the four 'intel inside' notes. All these have built awareness of brand to a point where they do not need to shout. You instinctively know. Tactical campaigns are designed to produce quick and quantifiable results; brand awareness simply builds the platform so that the tactical work is instantly recognisable as from a particular brand that has built trust over a number of years. That's half the battle! Your advertising has to be to the point. Too many ads in the B2B press try so hard to cram in the most amount of detail that the poor viewer does not know what to look at first! Net result is that they turn the page. It is estimated that you have exactly 1.7 seconds to grab attention before the prospect moves on to another page, so the advertising has to be instantly recognisable as from your brand. Be precise and simple. Less is more!

Brochures etc

Direct mail campaigns, below-the-line communications (basically anything that is classed as information – brochures, leaflets, price lists and the like), all need to follow a family feel, convey the brand ethos, and paint a consistent picture of your organisation.

As an example, many B2B engineering companies try very hard to produce exciting products, but give out boring literature that was first styled back in the eighties, and still looks like it! The corporate style needs to be kept updated. This may simply be by introducing better colours that differentiate you from your competitors or involve a completely new corporate identity. Just remember, a new identity is not your brand! What below-the-line literature does is back up and reinforce the advertising (which is known as above-the-line and is basically anything that is considered as advertising – TV, radio, and both local and national press ads). Below-the-line communications deliver the brand style more effectively than advertising in some ways because there is more of it, and when done well it is more personal and targeted. If it isn't done well, then it is not being effective in either producing results or enhancing the brand. If you use an external agency to produce this work, ensure you hold them to accountable for adhering to corporate style and your holistic brand strategy, as well as accuracy, quality and creativity. If they also have a strong brand ethos, then you will benefit from their attention to detail, and the service you receive.

Don't be fooled by creativity alone – you need great service and consistent quality to build your brand on a project-by-project basis, as well as proactive, creative approaches. You, not the agency, control the messages in line with the brand strategy and where you want to go in the future. It is your responsibility also to ensure the organisation is able to deliver whatever the brand messages promise!

Events, exhibitions and sponsorship

All of these may be suitable for your organisation, but they tend to be expensive and, unless done well, can do more harm to the brand than good. There is nothing worse than a badly designed 'shell scheme' stand at an exhibition, or exhibiting simply because the competition is also exhibiting. Consider carefully whether the brand message portrayed through a poor stand effectively represents what the brand values are, and whether you are enhancing or damaging the brand. Do it well, or don't do it at all. This is an area of implementation that really needs your control. Ensure the brief to the contractors meets the brand criteria (particularly if you are using a design company to design the graphics or a contractor to produce and erect the stand). Only staff the stand with personnel that will adequately reflect the levels of customer service you adhere to.

Sponsorship is a brand awareness issue, and should only be authorised where the brand will benefit from awareness to the right audience. This is particularly true for B2B rather than B2C companies where wider target audiences are the norm. There is little point sponsoring the local boys' football team (other than for altruistic motives expecting no return) if your target market is not local one.

Any local sponsorship, (particularly community-based projects) can have a longer-term benefit for future recruitment, if you rely a local workforce, or need to improve your visibility to the local community at large. Do not expect great sales returns from sponsorship, but it can play a part in building staff morale. We are not saying that charitable giving and local sponsorship are unimportant, because they are, but simply that such sponsorship normally assists perceptions much more than sales.

The same applies to green issues – portraying your green credentials not only helps ecologically, but it builds reputation as a responsible employer, which in turn assists recruitment. These perceptions build the brand, as well as saving the planet!

Building authority and gravitas

Whether you want to be seen as a market leader, an expert player in a specific market, or simply as someone who knows what they are talking about, then you need to build some level of authority. This comes over time and can be done in a variety of ways. We have discussed PR as one way – networking is another prime example of opportunities to build authority. Connecting with other potential customers, and issuing blogs and articles, all create authority and gravitas. For smaller companies, word-of-mouth advertising is of greater value than putting ads in Yellow Pages or on Yell.com. Why? Because your authority and expertise is enhanced through personal recommendation far better than what you say in an advertisement. For larger SME companies authority and gravitas can be enhanced by creativity and product innovation.

In any case, you need authority because it builds trust. Trust enhances sales opportunities and overrides price comparisons to a great extent. Authority and gravitas do not need to be boring and technical. It can be technical, but it can also be presented in such a way that it reflects the brand as exciting and forward-thinking (unless of course you want to build a less exciting and more conservative brand!). The key is consistently issuing authorative material, giving authorative advice, possibly giving seminars or presentations, and generally portraying authority and gravitas through all levels of internal/external communication.

Summary

The way you handle the sum total of each of these areas becomes an important factor in differentiating your organisation from a host of others. This is holistic branding. It is what makes your Unique Selling Propositions (USPs) into tangible experiences for all stakeholders. The benefits are so enormous we wonder why holistic branding isn't better recognised by the B2B sector. Align all departments, processes, procedures and training to go in a single direction according to the brand strategy, and you will inevitably make the customers return again and again. A caveat to this, of course, is that even the best aligned brand strategy will not compensate for poor quality products or services.

a great brand **doesn't** compensate for poor products

Keeping it going

So many projects start with an initial enthusiasm, only for obstacles, financial challenges and lack of buy-in to bring them down to a painfully slow pace, if they do not stop altogether. A leader does not accept failure. The ability to envision others will bring people with them to a higher level, but it has to be maintained and pushed further every day. Remember that every change in personnel in the future has the potential to make a negative impact on the brand — unless the brand is so well organised in every department that all personnel changes simply enhance the brand.

The key to keeping it going is to constantly keep the brand manifesto in view. The brand manifesto contains all you need to make it work as long as it has life within the organisation. The moment it becomes either an imposed regime or a piece of work that was once strictly followed, but is now partially disregarded, then the brand slips and the problems multiply. The brand manifesto is a living dynamic that may adapt, but never depart from the direction without a conscious decision by the board to do so. This is a strategy, not a Magna Carta once-only proclamation. It's the American Constitution – it can have amendments!

This takes us back full circle to the beginning of this chapter – who is going to keep your brand maintained and going forward? Someone has to be in control of it. That person has to believe in it, live it, see the benefits of it, and be able to enthuse others of those benefits. As we said at the beginning of the book – this isn't rocket science. It is just common sense!

Chapter 6
Tangible and intangible benefits

We have clearly demonstrated that building a strong brand works. We have been through the theory and the practical implementation of how to begin, and how to maintain it. There are many benefits you can expect from putting all this into practice as you build a holistic brand. The list at the end of this chapter can act as a reminder for you when things are tough, not gelling, or when your employees still don't get it! It may even be a good idea to let all personnel have a copy (translated into your corporate style of course!) so they can see what their part is achieving.

However, for business owners, venture capitalists or MDs who want to move on and up, the biggest benefit will be realised when the time comes to consider, and plan for, an exit route.

The long-term benefit of brand equity

Brand equity is seen by accountants as an intangible element. Over and above assets, a company can build 'goodwill' into a business sale. However, goodwill is not straightforward because it is nebulous. Dictionary definitions of goodwill in an accounting sense state: **Goodwill:** *'an intangible asset valued according to the advantage or reputation a business has acquired (over and above its tangible assets).'*

Another definition states: *'the value of a business that is beyond the market value of any tangible assets. It includes reputation, prestige, and company name.'*

Way back in 1901, on 20 May in the House of Lords, a senior judge, Lord MacNaghten answered this question: *'What is goodwill? It is a thing very easy to describe, very difficult to define. It is the benefit and advantage of the good name, reputation and connection of a business. It is the attractive force which brings in custom. It is the one thing which distinguishes an old-established business from a new business at its first start.'*[1]

These early attempts to clarify what makes goodwill led to a definition in a court case in 1934. The case of Whiteman Smith Motor Co. Ltd. v Chaplin, led the court to define goodwill, and the relationship between location and customer loyalty. The court found that customers have different habits and characteristics, and that an analogy could be drawn from the habits and behaviours of animals. This definition has become known as the Zoological classification, and we will explain this a bit later.

goodwill **is not** straightforward because it is nebulous

There are some recognised industries (such as the farming industry and not-for-profit organisations) where goodwill is not relevant because there is no need of the traditional customer loyalty definitions. For the vast majority of companies, however, at the end of the day, a business is only worth what someone is prepared to pay for it.

The sale of assets without goodwill brings very little return – we all know that second-hand equipment isn't worth a lot! This is why goodwill is so important in a sale. It is the intangible element that produces the real value for the seller and real benefits for the acquirer. So it seems unwise to leave this element of a business sale as open to opinion and negotiation.

Generally, goodwill is seen as just one item, but not by accountants. In order to asses the value of goodwill, and what factors are important, accountants divide the goodwill into three components:

- Locational (or inherent) goodwill
- Personal goodwill
- Company (or free) goodwill

Locational goodwill obviously refers to where a company is situated. So for a hotel sited next to a motorway junction, or a restaurant set on the beach front, locational goodwill would play a major part in defining what the goodwill element of a sale could be. This calculation would be based both on regular customer base and there would also be some element included to allow for passing customer traffic. If ,on the other hand, the company is manufacturing products which sell worldwide, and are distributed from some industrial estate, then location would play only a very small part in the calculations. Locational goodwill determines whether the customers are loyal because of the location, or stay because of the reputation or products of the company. If the business were to be relocated, would it retain its customer base or have to find a new set of customers? What would the value be when the cost to replace customers that leave has been taken into consideration?

Personal goodwill is based on the personality, reputation and abilities of an individual (or individuals). For example, where most of the customer contacts are generated through a personal network (particularly that of the owner) then again the question arises of where the customer loyalty lies — in the owner or the business? Would customers leave because the owner is no longer around? Another factor is that, as well as key customer contacts, very often the technical competencies and skill sets also lie with key personnel. Acquirers need to assess the likelihood of key personnel departing on change of ownership and the ramifications of such departures. So personal goodwill provides yet another imponderable in exit calculations.

Company goodwill lies in a customer's trust in the company. This is obviously much more in the area of brand reputation and brand loyalty. It is affected more by products and services offered, and the perception of quality surrounding such offerings. The customer is attracted primarily to the name of the company or product, not to the owner or the location, which are unimportant factors. However, this is seen only as one factor to be included and balanced against the other goodwill factors.

All these three elements of goodwill are based on the traditional model of customers dictating the price, as well as the reputation of a company, and therefore playing major part of the profitability of a business. It was therefore necessary to define the types of customer that a business has, in order to fit them into one or more parts of the above goodwill components.

Returning to the Whiteman Smith Motor Co. Ltd. v Chaplin case of 1934, the court gave these definitions of customers and their loyalty patterns:

- the dog, who stays faithful to the person and not the location
- the cat, who stays faithful to the location and not the person
- the rabbit, who comes because it is close and for no other reason
- the rat, who is casual and is attracted to neither person nor location

The first type of customer, the dog, applies especially to small businesses such as photographers or the building trades such as plasterers, tilers, etc., where much of the skill and expertise is vested in one person. Customers like the person's style, their work ethics and their reputation. This definition concerns not necessarily just one-man-bands, but also businesses where the name of the company includes the name of the owner (for example, Paul Pipe Plumbers Ltd.) where the service or product remains highly connected to a personality.

The second type of customer, the cat, is not based on loyalty to one personality. This type of customer is drawn to the location, for example, a restaurant. They are a customer of the business because its location suits their lifestyle choices or business requirements. This is much more apparent in the B2C sector because it is often reliant on a specific location (as smaller high street retailers, for example). Move a shop, lose the passing trade. Move a plumbers merchant (B2B) anywhere in the area and the customer base is hardly affected.

The third type, the rabbit, uses the business only because it is convenient. If the business changed hands they would still be a customer. If the business changed in nature, then they would find the nearest business that replicated the offering of the original company. An example of this could be customers of a hire outlet of some kind who need to hire a piece of equipment, so nearest is probably one of the major factors why they choose to be a customer.

Finally, we have the rat. These customers have no loyalty. They often sniff around, smell out the best deal and buy on price rather than on personality, reputation or location. This puts them much more clearly in the B2B sector (local stationery suppliers are a good example where customers primarily buy on price alone). Rats are not the type of customer you can easily retain after the first sale.

140

Obviously there are overlaps between the definitions. The challenge for accountants is to successfully leverage the most important factors to achieve the sale, whilst minimising the other factors that could reduce the value. This balancing act is subject to a whole host of opinions and counter-opinions, with both sides trying to do the best on behalf of their clients. The fact that all these calculations are based on customer loyalty (or lack of), therefore leaves much room for interpretation. It engenders no confidence for either the seller or the acquirer because the valuation is eventually agreed by what they believe the customer base may or may not do. The difference between the goodwill method of valuation and a brand equity valuation is stark.

The key lies in eliminating the variables so that a much clearer picture of the future is available to the acquirer. Essentially, by building a holistic brand over a period of time you can control the types of customers that an organisation attracts – and more importantly, retains. You will be able to demonstrate a continuity of earnings pattern that is sustainable after exit. You can prove that the business will retain its customer base because of the way the organisation behaves, interacts and influences the market.

Reducing the number of uncertainties involved with goodwill valuations involves influencing customers: those who are loyal because of location (cats), customers who were attracted to an individual personality (dogs), and the customers who are only attracted by convenience (rabbits). Some rats will continue to be rats! Building loyal customers based on the brand, not on a single personality or a few key individuals, puts that loyalty where most value can be gained. Perhaps a new analogy needs to be added to the Zoological classification – the horse!

Horse and rider

The horse is able to be ridden and therefore requires a degree of influence by the rider. It was also one of the first animals to be branded by its owner! Although a horse can react particularly to its owner, it is not solely loyal to that owner, and can be ridden by any other rider. It is, therefore, unlike the dog, which does not reliably respond to the directions of anyone other than its owner (or trainer). When ridden correctly there is a 'oneness' between horse and rider where the horse instinctively responds to the lightest of signals. Such is the rapport that the experience is great for both the rider and the horse. The horse is not loyal to a location (like the cat is), nor comes just because you are close (like the rabbit) – ever tried catching a horse when it doesn't want to be bridled? Lastly, horses do not scavenge (like rats). No, they like to be free, but also love to be ridden and controlled.

Strong brands control the experiences and perceptions of their customers by implementing a holistic brand strategy, thus creating a horse and rider synergy that brings benefits to both. Dog-like customers therefore become horses, cat customers become horses, rabbits become horses, and even some rats become horses!

Where you only have horses, you have controlled customer loyalty. When you control customer loyalty you have a valuable, tangible brand that is well positioned for future growth. That's brand equity!

How to assess brand equity

A number of efforts have been made to recognise brand equity as a separate entity within the report and accounts, particularly during the internet boom period a few years ago. Many companies were sold on the speculative premise that the customer base would be sustainable in the future. Inadvisably these companies were then valued on the

brand

=

€quity

strength of their brand name without any financial certainty to back up the prospect of future growth through customer loyalty. The internet bubble burst, and this has led many accountants to believe that this method of calculating the value of a business does not work.

However, it is possible to identify brand equity. This can be demonstrated quite clearly with major global B2C brands such as Intel, Kodak, Marks & Spencer and many others. For example, a company such as Amazon continues to flourish in the internet arena. Do customers care who runs the company? Do they want to visit because it's close? Do they care where the headquarters are? No. All they care about is the customer care they receive – whether the books arrive in good time and in good condition. The true value of Amazon is therefore entirely in its reputation – not in a location or a personality. The brand equity can, therefore, be quite clearly demonstrated as a tangible asset because the value of the company is not in its physical assets, but in its reputation and customer loyalty. If Amazon was ever to be valued for disposal or acquisition, future sales patterns would not be affected (provided that the same levels of customer care continued). The ability to sustain future turnover through customer loyalty is the key factor – this is what makes brand equity.

So we need to apply some measurements in order to arrive at a brand equity figure that can be used as a hard factor in the valuation of a business:
- Sound financial data
- Brand strength against competitors
- Influence on customers and markets

Firstly, there has to be sound financial data over a period of, say, 5 years in order to form a base on which to separate the intangible earnings (patents, management expertise, etc.) of the organisation from the tangible assets (equipment and materials, etc.). The value of the business must not be in a personality or a location, but have been deliberately and consistently embedded into the very core of the organisation.

Secondly, we need to look at how strong the brand is against its competitors. Is the brand at risk (for example, by competitor product innovation) or has it gained an advantage (for instance, by introducing new products or by delivering better customer experiences)? The stronger the brand, the more accurately future earnings can be predicted, because the risk of not achieving those figures is minimised. A weaker brand may have more difficulty in achieving the same growth because it has a harder job persuading customers to remain loyal.

Lastly, we have to assess how much the brand is influencing its customer base – is retention strong and sustainable? How much is the brand influencing customer demand? Strong brands use marketing to find customer needs and fill the gap, therefore creating greater demand. Weak brands just jump on a bandwagon. If you can see the bandwagon then you're already too late to market and you're playing catch up (me too businesses). Of course, if you can exploit a gap in the market so much the better! So customer and market influence is another key factor when estimating future revenue.

This is why holistic branding brings such a competitive edge. If every area of an organisation is viewed as affecting the whole brand, then there will be clear evidence that all three criteria are measurable. Where this is possible, then you can easily assess what the financial value of the brand is, not affected by personalities, locations, or even product price!

So brand equity can be assessed, and is more clear-cut than the traditional 'goodwill' model. Accountants may still want to call that goodwill (because they understand the terminology), but if you can take out the uncertainties in predicting future earnings, then actually you can demonstrate real brand equity!

The more immediate benefits

You may not be thinking of an exit strategy in the immediate future, but that should not stop you beginning to build for that event now. There are numerous tangible benefits to be gained along the way by putting a holistic brand strategy together and implementing it daily. In fact, banks are much more willing to be co-operative when the going gets rough, if they know there is:

- a viable strategy in place to improve the business
- a management team committed to do what it says it will
- a defined set of targets that are being achieved
- a positive culture emerging
- a differentiated business with clear potential

Too many companies leave it far too late before taking action to prevent downturn or even liquidation. Bad management is nearly always to blame, but management teams often do not want to face up to their responsibilities in an ethical manner soon enough. Building a holistic brand strategy, and then implementing it day-by-day, can only help to prevent a business from performing badly. It will not prevent bad management. As we said right at the beginning of this book, the fundamental key to building a holistic brand lies in the boardroom. When brand is put back into the boardroom, then you have every chance of influencing the outcome and preventing bad management at all levels, because direction and purpose are clearly defined.

Chapter 7
Undertaking a simple brand diagnostic

The first step to building a brand strategy is a thorough brand diagnosis – a snapshot of where an organisation is failing, or succeeding, in building a cohesive brand. However, this is not a 'one-size-fits-all' model. Although your business may be in a crowded marketplace with products and services very similar to others, it is unique in many ways, particularly if you delve 'below the waterline'. The internal culture, deeply-held company values, and employee morale will all be different from your competitors, as will your visual identity, and product offerings.

The concept of the brand model[1] was developed from the fact that most brands are based primarily on only one or two of the four areas. Normally those areas are talents and voice which tend to be the more visible areas of business. But it is only in ensuring that all four areas correlate with each other, that a truly complete brand can be built.

A brand diagnostic is not designed to give answers to any issues. It is designed specifically to highlight where organisational disconnects are happening. When we understand where these disconnects are, then we can begin to address the most pressing issues. This will help to develop a brand strategy that will ultimately improve the bottom line. There are many resources available that deal with all areas of business, but if tackled in isolation from each other, the disconnects will continue to the detriment of the brand. Negative perceptions and experiences will continue to flourish, unchecked and unresolved, in a downward spiral. Once you have undertaken your own brand diagnostic, it will become obvious which areas need tackling first.

[1] *See chapter 2 for the brand model*

The following twenty statements form the basis of a simple, but effective, brand diagnostic, and the explanations of each statement will assist you in understanding where disconnects could be occurring in your organisation. You will find a diagnostic scorecard in appendix 1 at the end of the book. We suggest you photocopy the scorecard so you can fill it in as you go through the questions in this chapter, or pass the scorecard on to your colleagues to gain a more accurate picture of the state of your brand as it stands now.

don't

cheat

by checking how the scoring works!

When you have finished and collated the questions you will be able to check how your company brand scored by checking your score against the diagnostic evaluation in appendix 2. Don't cheat and check how the scoring works before you do the diagnostic — you just won't get a true picture of where you are! As we said right at the beginning — most companies don't operate holistically, so there's no guilt attached, whatever your result shows. The important thing is to be as realistic as possible so you can understand where you really are, and then you can move on to solving some of the more pressing issues with confidence. Measure your answers by using this score key. Have fun!

Score key

1	Strongly disagree
2	Inclined to disagree
3	Neither agree nor disagree
4	Inclined to agree
5	Strongly agree

1	We have a clear sense of mission that is shared by everyone in the organisation

For many people in business, purpose is misrendered as a mission statement. But mission speaks primarily of an activity to be undertaken (go on a mission, a mission to mars, etc.) It will probably state what the company does, and how it will do it, rather than why it does what it does. Purpose is much more about the intention to proceed in a certain manner, in line with a set of values and principles.

Have you stopped and asked yourself 'why the heck are we doing this?' What is the real reason — is it just for the money? There's almost certainly a deeper motivational force that lies behind why an organisation does what it does. It could be that they love helping people, or advancing technology for the benefit of mankind, or a desire to ecologically save the planet. The real purpose is the base on which to build vision as much as core values are.

The statement implies that the common purpose is understood at all levels within the organisation. The board members may have a clear and common purpose, but could that purpose be succinctly explained in the office or on the shop floor? If the workforce can't comprehend the real reason why the organisation is in business, how can they understand why they should help to fulfil the vision?

Teasing out the core purpose of why a company does what it does, will provide vastly greater clarity than any stand-alone mission statement, and it will bolster the vision and the things valued. Do not undervalue purpose — it pays to understand the why.

The key to answering this statement accurately is: Is it shared by everyone?

score

2   The organisation is quick to learn from both successes and failures

Behind the formation of every company there was (or is) a visionary whose zeal and enthusiasm got the whole thing off the ground before any responses to circumstances began to formulate a pathway to the present. It is revealing to discover how much the current board understands about the history of the organisation – what the greatest drivers have been towards the present, which obstacles have been overcome so the company moved forward, and which obstacles held it back. It is all too possible that a past failure in one area restricts attempting a similar move again, albeit that there are now different personalities, products, processes, and market conditions prevailing. Sometimes we just 'throw the baby out with the bathwater'.

So how quick is the organisation in building on successes and communicating those successes throughout the organisation? How quickly do you adjust to failure, and what response to failure do you have? Has your company repeated the same mistakes again, or are there now processes in place to avoid the pitfalls?

The key to answering this statement accurately is: Can you quantify this?

score

| 3 | We regularly review our reputation with our customers, our suppliers and our staff |

Who controls an organisation's reputation? There are two scenarios here — the first is that a company allows its customers' perceptions, (both good and bad) to influence that reputation. This is costly, and is becoming much more so in this age of internet communication. A few years ago, one disgruntled customer could probably have been managed because communication was more or less limited to verbal discussions with a few of his or her acquaintances — and there it probably stopped. No great fuss then, as long as you didn't have too many disgruntled customers the reputation wasn't badly affected.

Not so now. The age of the internet has dawned, and a single 'blog' can be seen by millions around the world within hours. Other people tell of like experiences — even small matters assume great significance — and vilification grows rapidly. Businesses can no longer afford to leave their reputation in the hands of customers, ex-employees or suppliers. We have seen it written that 'brand is no longer managed from the top' (meaning that it is now managed solely by customer perception). This couldn't be more wrong, or more costly.

The second scenario is just the opposite: Brand must be managed from the top! Managing a brand holistically will ensure that what is lived within the organisation will also be portrayed in its dealings with customers. Customers aren't fooled by mere messages — they experience the brand. Or they look on the net, they research, and they check blogs before making a decision. If everything out there isn't good, they'll know, and people moan about it much more than they will extol your virtues. All of this means business leaders must be aware of the communication and technology revolution we are living through. Bad news travels very fast these days — and hangs around forever. Once it's out there, it's there to stay, and if it's there, it can be found!

The good news is that if a brand is really managed 'from the top down' then the chances of negative feedback are minimised — happy customers don't blog bad news! You may believe that you have a good reputation — but do you really know? Reputation is often assumed, based on 'gut feelings' not based on structured research.

The key to answering this statement accurately is: With all three groups?

score

<table>
<tr><td>4</td><td>Our staff can articulate the differences between our organisation and our competitors</td></tr>
</table>

We have already made the case that every business venture is unique. It is these differences that set you apart from the competition, but if they are measurable and understood, leverage can be brought to bear in order to gain a competitive advantage. These differentiators can be both internal and external. What makes your organisation different to others? It may be easy for top management to articulate these differentiators, but this may not be so easy for other personnel.

External differentiators here speak of products and services, much more than visual differences in corporate style. Internal differentiators include the working environment, staff welfare and benefits – the various reasons why people want to work for a company. We all hope it isn't just for the money, or that it's close to where they live. Both of these may be a factor, but most people have emotional reasons for staying if you dig deep enough. Have they been asked? Why should they be asked? We need to ask because it concerns people's likes and dislikes (personality) and their interaction with customers and suppliers (talents). Would the differences that top management articulate be the same as those articulated by the warehouse staff or the office junior? You may know what the differences are... do they?

The key to answering this statement accurately is: Sure about all staff?

score

Principles are the line the organisation won't cross. They are the things you hold most sacred – no compromise! Principles are foundational, because we're talking about the integrity of character. These principles must be evident to everyone in order to control every company action. This is one of the main areas where a brand can be seriously damaged, particularly if the company personnel are caught out in breach of the stated principles. Principles should control behaviour throughout the organisation – but are you sure?

Remember Enron, the giant oil company? They had 'integrity' as one of their core values:

'We work with customers and prospects openly, honestly and sincerely. When we say we will do something, we will do it; when we say we cannot or will not do something, then we won't do it.'[2]

Embedded within this value statement is the implied principle 'we will not be dishonest'. Oh yes? What Enron is now infamously cited for is its bankruptcy (moral and financial) resulting from a huge embezzlement scandal, with shady wheeling and dealing, and huge sums disappearing into 'black holes'. All this resulted in prison sentences for some the top Enron management team for fraudulent activities. Unfortunately, the world is littered with organisations that have failed in the eyes of their customers, or when the gaze of public scrutiny unearths a tasty story of immoral, unethical, or unsavoury behaviour.

The key to answering this statement accurately is: Never? Can you be sure?

score

[2] *Extract from the Enron Vision and Values Statement*

6   Personnel at all levels are excited about the direction the organisation is taking

Most companies already have, or been told that they should have, a vision statement. The trouble is that most traditional vision and mission statements do not include any of the emotional elements of a business, and even if they do, they only tell a superficial, isolated part of the story. But the biggest problem is that they are almost always created as separate tasks; they are not seen as a single entity within a larger picture, and therefore lack any meaningful assistance to building a holistic brand strategy. Unless the values, purpose, and background of the enterprise are clearly thought through first, it will not be possible to package them together into a meaningful brand strategy that can inspire the entire organisation.

The point of this statement is to assess the level of optimism at board level, and then consider the percentage of people within the organisation that you feel would share the same level of optimism. If there's a big difference it could highlight a communication issue that needs to be addressed. The same should be applied to the performance of the organisation – is it static, moving forward slowly, or really heading towards the vision? The board will have one belief, but is the belief the same in the office and on the shop floor?

The key to answering this statement accurately is: How do you know?

score

Motivated personnel are always the key ingredient in building a holistic brand, and a positive culture is the 'natural bonding' that allows this to develop. Gaining buy-in to the brand manifesto is the starting point, and ensures you are building a great working environment that engenders motivation. There will be other areas which need attention to bed down the concept of building the brand holistically. You may need to reassess your communication channels, because lack of good communication will hinder the creation of a new culture across all departments. You may need to instigate a new slant on your recruitment policies in order to begin to build a team that 'fits' the brand culture you desire, but whichever starting point is chosen, it will not be the last. No brand will become strong enough until all the stones in the dry stone wall of your organisation fit together as one, held by a common, cohesive, organisational culture.

Exceptional performance stems from motivation, and motivation is bolstered by recognition. Many organisations do this in an ad hoc manner, but a structured appraisal system is far better. Structured training, together with recognition of achievement through a performance-related pay structure, are extremely motivating, but even more motivating is public recognition (both for individuals and teams) for a job well done. Rewards need not be expressly financially — just as memorable may be paying for an employee to take his/her partner to a restaurant! If regular performance recognition is not built into your culture as a part of the brand strategy, it should be!

The key to answering this statement accurately is:
Is recognition and motivation structured?

score

8 Working practices in the organisation have changed as a result of market trends

All organisations need to change with the times — the question is how? This statement requires balance. There is the danger that an organisation becomes so inward focused that it can lose the bigger picture of what is happening around it. Attitudes that amount to 'we've always done it that way' or 'we have always got decent results in the past' amount to the prospect of haphazard change, stifled growth potential or worse still, no progress at all.

However, change for change's sake is unprofitable as well. Change is a constant, but it needs to be managed change in order to remain in line with the brand strategy, so the concept of constant change must be built into your culture. Proactive change is strategic, reactive change is tactical and you need to determine which is required and at what point in time so that customer expectations are always exceeded.

The key to answering this statement accurately is: How well is change managed?

score

All companies wish to maintain or increase their market share, and in order to do this, healthy businesses find their niche markets. This is not about whether the organisation is the market leader or number one hundred in the pecking order. This statement reflects brand strength or brand weakness.

What is the market worth? This is much more about measurable increase, rather than 'gut feel' or the fact that the turnover has increased. Is the market increasing or decreasing? Can you quantify your market share compared to your competitors? Which of the competition has increased or decreased as a result of market changes? If you can't answer this easily, then do some research – even a basic estimate will bring benefits when building and implementing the strategy.

The key to answering this statement accurately is: Can you prove it?

score

10 Our recuitment policy has been developed as a result of work undertaken on our vision and values

As business leaders we have strong views about the sort of person the organisation should employ. Traditionally companies hired more on skill-sets than on attitude. Companies need to realise how important attitude is — you can teach skills, but it's almost impossible to change character — and a lot more complicated to disinfect the company! Negative characters, people who aren't team players, unambitious people — all infect others. Worst is hiring someone only to discover that it was 'just another job on the career ladder'.

For example, if one of the core values is passion, then the company needs to hire people with passion to inspire others around them. It is far more important to hire someone who 'fits' the brand, than just take on people because they can do the job role. Additionally, if an organisation has an openly defined culture based on clearly understood brand strategy, it can positively enhance the recruitment opportunities when the word on the street is 'that's a great place to work!' That happens because all the employees say it is, so even if your company is in the micro section of SMEs (companies with less than ten employees), it is still imperative to hire people who fit a predetermined attitude/character profile.

Furthermore, if there is a structured induction process, does it include an introduction to the culture of the organisation? There is no better way to get a new staff member conversant with the company culture from the very outset than to immerse them in it from day one. Training of this depth is highly valued by those organisations that have taken on board the 'Investors in People' training model. Such a training methodology will greatly assist in building a holistic brand because ultimately personnel attitudes will directly affect the perceptions and experiences of the brand.

The key to answering this statement accurately is: Based on vision and values?

score

11 We have a very low staff turnover rate

Different market sectors have differing levels of 'acceptable' staff turnover, and all companies experience growth and churn in the area of recruitment. The key is not only getting the right people, but keeping them. Whatever market you are in, if you have a strong holistic brand, your staff turnover will be lower than average because your internal culture will be good. But how can prospective employees buy into a brand culture unless it is clearly distinguishable both internally and externally?

You can achieve extraordinary results with ordinary people, if you recruit the right team. Teamwork overpowers individual brilliance virtually every time. As Cisco's CEO John Chambers says, *'if you're going to empower people and you don't have teamwork, you're dead'.* He should know – most companies in that sector have a staff turnover approaching 30%... Cisco's is now just 8%. If we look at one of Cisco's core value statements we can begin to understand why…

'One of the core values at Cisco is empowering people to empower themselves. It serves as the basis of how Cisco is organized, for both our corporate structure and our corporate culture. We have learned that one important component of employee satisfaction is the feeling on the part of employees that their company is investing in their communities, and supportive of the lives of community members outside the office.' [3]

[3]   *www.cisco.com*

So tying the recruitment policy into the brand strategy is one of the fundamental elements in building a holistic brand. The next step is to form a 'natural bonding' by creating a positive, excited, dynamic internal culture. Basing the recruitment policy on a predetermined profile will help to ensure that there is a 'fit' with the brand. Keeping your staff is then much easier because you have the right personality to begin with. Maintaining an internal culture permeated by a common vision, as well as the usual employee benefit schemes and staff welfare, will inevitably reduce staff turnover.

The key to answering this statement accurately is: Can you quantify very low?

score

12   We regularly review our product placement strategy

Products loom large in the B2B portfolio, naturally because that's where profitability is conventionally generated. We live in a world of features and specifications, deadlines and delivery, technical wizardry through R&D, and engage in the pursuit of the holy grail of uniqueness every business day. We are so ruled by these things that we lose sight (if we ever perceived it) of what a brand really is, and the value that a strong brand strategy brings.

Many companies in the B2B sector consider themselves service industries, but although services rendered do not necessarily have the tangibility of an engineered product set, they are just as vulnerable to customer perceptions and expectations. Software products and business consultancy are classic examples of this. This is why perceptions and expectations rule every time. Modern marketing theory is now based much more on finding what a target audience requires, and then developing and creating products or services to meet those requirements. In so doing, they create yet more perceptions and expectations together with the inbuilt potential for affecting the brand positively or negatively.

A conventional and commonly accepted marketing model is based on the traditional 4 Ps of the marketing mix – Product, Price, Place and Promotion, and positions brand as a subset of the marketing strategy. Even though modern marketing theory increases those 4 Ps to 7 or 8, they all place the product as king. In the holistic brand it is experience that is king! Because experiences and perceptions govern a brand, not the product set, then a holistic brand strategy must direct all areas – including the marketing strategy. Branding is not a function of marketing – marketing is a function of branding!

When was the last time you reviewed your products in comparison to your competitors? How do you know if your product placement is right unless you review your marketing strategy in line with your brand strategy?

The key to answering this statement accurately is: Against a bigger strategy?

score

13 Our product support differs significantly from that of our competitors

Most B2B companies place great emphasis on product differentiation, but often product support has very little differentiation as it is 'much of a muchness'. However, because experience of a brand is king, not simply the product, this is an area where many organisations can gain a great advantage.

You can have great product warranties, great user-friendly product manuals, maintain a 'clean' CRM database, but all of these can be destroyed by a single bad experience from the help desk. If a customer's experience of the organisation is poor, then all the hard work, all the investment in R&D, all your marketing campaigns, will be wasted. Back you go to the stadium getting new customers all over again.

Product support has be more than just the obvious, so answer the statement in light of this.

The key to answering this statement accurately is: Significantly?

score

14 We regularly review the factors that influence our customers' buying decisions

Too many B2B companies assume they know why their customers buy from them, and often these are not the real reasons at all. Even though purchasing involves rational thought processes, in the final analysis, a sales decision is essentially emotional. Trust, experience and the opinions of others all influence that decision, either negatively or positively.

Keeping up with trends, undertaking customer research, and evaluating your own research are all important factors in running a successful business. Find out what affects purchasing decisions – it can vary from pure economics, tribalism (wanting to 'belong'), and even prestige. The underlying thought behind the old IBM slogan 'no one ever got fired for buying an IBM' was about trust and reputation rather than product specifications.

Understand what your customers buy, over what you are selling. They may not actually be buying the product bells and whistles at all, they could be buying another six months in their job!

The key to answering this statement accurately is: Do you ask them?

score

15 We are happy with our current customer retention levels

Growth and churn are inherent for every business, but as everyone knows, it's a lot easier and cheaper to keep a good customer than it is to get a new one. If you're not happy with retention levels, there could be a mixture of reasons why you lose customers. It could be your internal culture is not as positive as you think. Are your staff encouraged to think 'outside the box' of policy rules and regulations in order to solve a customer's problem? It could be down to price (in which case your brand is not very strong), but it's more likely to be that you haven't correctly communicated the value-for-money proposition. How about the marketing strategy – is it in line with a brand strategy or is it doing its own thing? This is a straight-forward statement, but one that could highlight a number of areas for improvement.

You could be best at picking up new customers, but if you lose customers on a regular basis you have a disconnect. Whatever the cause (for example, because you don't meet their needs, talk to them in the wrong way, at an inappropriate level, or your service levels are poor), then it's back to the stadium again!

The key to answering this statement accurately is: Could it be better?

score

This statement is obviously linked to the last statement, but the areas for improvement may not be the same. The quality of the CRM database is vital — is it kept constantly up-to-date, or are you still mailing out-of-date contacts? Are you complying with Data Protection and Telephone Preference Service regulations?

Your delivery and dispatch procedures can be another area where customer service can fail, as can the speed of response to enquiries, phone calls and emails. Does the entire organisation have the same values and principles to underpin customer service? To remind you again, all of these areas are related to, and held together by, a positive, customer-focused, 'can-do' internal culture. If you fail in one area of customer service, it will be undermining other good areas.

The key to answering this statement accurately is: How connected is it?

score

17 Our pricing strategy is driven more by our reputation than by other factors

Developing a strategy of holistic branding can effectively ease a business away from price-based offerings, into value-based offerings, because customers do not buy solely on price – they buy value, benefits and trust. Unless you are actively trying to be the cheapest in the market, there is actually no such thing as 'cheap' or 'expensive' – only the perception of value-for-money. That value can be leveraged through holistic branding – not simply good packaging or good marketing (although both may be important), but through building a reputation for added value and trust that sets a company apart from everyone else. A strong brand reputation should drive the pricing strategy, not the tactical campaigns produced by your competitors. Even though a company must take note, through research, of what the market can accept, pricing strategy has to be consistently in line with your reputation.

Take an example from the proverbial widget manufacturer. The basic pricing strategy would cover factors such as material costs, labour costs, overheads, etc. Let's just call this Cost.

Therefore:
(Cost + profit margin) – discounts = price

But:
(Cost + profit margin) + brand reputation = higher price

This is particularly true of training and consultancy pricing – you do not just buy 'hours taken' (costs), you buy on the expertise they have, on the potential benefits they will bring (value), and on the reputation of the consultant or consultancy.

So if your pricing strategy is driven by a strong brand reputation, then profitability should be increasing, because reputation can gain a tangible pricing advantage! This statement assists in indicating the current strength or weakness of the brand reputation.

The key to answering this statement accurately is: How do you know the level of reputation?

score

18 | Our customers believe that we deliver value-for-money

What value does the customer derive from doing business with an organisation? Value is a tangible element if it is clear to the customer that they are not just 'paying the negotiated price'.

As an example from the B2C world, ask yourself why it is that people pay more for clothes from well-known brand names, rather than buy cheaper, non-branded clothes of the same quality? The answer is, that although these products are tribal (it says something about a person's taste and values, and that they subconsciously want to 'belong'), it is also because customers are prepared to pay extra for perceived quality engendered through the reputation of the brand (added value). It can be the same in B2B — customers don't buy products solely on price — they buy on a host of other factors, which include after sales warranties, CRM, reliability, delivery times, etc., all of which are founded on an organisation's good reputation and their customers' trust in it. All things being equal, sales are finally more emotional than rational.

Additionally, long-term relationships where a customer's needs are fully understood, met or exceeded every time, can also create value, both for the customer and the supplier. All organisations deal with various suppliers, but far and away the most important factor in choosing (and continuing to use) a supplier, is that the supplier provides a consistent quality service that can be relied on time and again. Suppliers that meet this criterion (among others) tend to get the work — even if it's a slightly higher rate, because integrity and consistency are highly valued. Reliability of this type protects the purchasing company's brand reputation with their own customers. Where trust has been carefully nurtured and maintained at all levels over a period of time, there are considerable emotional benefits to the purchaser.

The question to be answered here is, how do you know what your customers believe? You may think you deliver value-for-money, but do they? When was the last time you asked the question?

The key to answering this statement accurately is: How do you know?

score

19 Our profit margins are increasing

Why do people buy from you? Many B2B markets tend to be price-led and price-conscious by default – dependant on competitor pricing models. Downward market trends, shareholder expectations and the like, all produce a climate based around tactical marketing. This ever increasing cost-cutting causes compression of profitability for many, and we can get to a point where we ask, 'is it worth doing at all?'

To understand this statement we are not looking just at improved processes, smarter working, or cost-cutting. Again we are looking holistically at the entire organisation, because a holistic brand strategy will bring improvements in all areas including productivity, lower absenteeism, higher quality recruitment, a more positive culture and improvements in brand reputation, among a host of other benefits.

Look outside the box for this one. If profit is increasing, is it because the organisation is better connected and has improved against the competition, or because you have instigated stringent measures to protect the bottom line because the market-dictated price is so competitive?

**The key to answering this statement accurately is:
If they have, why have they?**

Most organisations have a marketing budget of some kind, and undertake a variety of marketing activities – the usual suspects being advertising, PR, website, direct mail and print. However, there are now many more channels to market, such as blogging, viral email campaigns and e-newsletters to name just a few. All of these need careful monitoring through response mechanisms/tracking codes on advertising, 'click-through' results and other analyses from internet activities, but how much do you really understand about the results you are getting?

As in all holistic branding areas, this needs to be based on long-term strategic analysis as well as short-term tactical monitoring. It is essential to know whether or not your marketing budget is working towards your goals, rather than why it's working. It assists in a controlled response rate rather than a reactive one.

It will pay to delve deeper if you can, to ascertain the ROI on all marketing activities and then adjust where necessary in light of other brand areas (such as reputation). Ensure all areas are producing the same messages.

The key to answering this statement accurately is: How accurately?

score

Conclusion

It will now be fairly obvious why brand should be holistic; each area being affected by others, or affecting other areas. Obviously this is not a full brand diagnostic, but it will provide a very good indicator of how connected your brand is at the moment, where you are stronger, and where there are areas for improvement.

Now add together all your scores and then turn to appendix 2 to get an assessment of the level of holistic branding you have achieved to date. Unless you have completed all the questions in this chapter, the next chapter won't make any sense because we then begin to cross-reference one answer against another to identify where your disconnects may be occurring.

Chapter 8
Identifying the disconnects

We have made the case that every business organisation is different, much like the analogy of the dry stone wall. Each stone represents one facet or area of the company, each held in place by the 'natural bonding' of the culture that permeates the organisation.

don't
leave it to

chance

We have stated that this 'natural bonding' does not occur by imposing a culture, but rather by continually working on the culture until it becomes so ingrained within the organisation that it becomes outworked naturally. Where all parts of an organisation feel fully involved, have the same desire to fulfil the company vision, and all have the same responses to setbacks and challenges, there is a strong brand!

But what happens when one part of the organisation is not so involved; does not share in the vision? What happens when a customer receives differing responses each time they come into contact with the business? What is the end result of inadvertently varying the underlying brand message (not meaning tactical messages) that the organisation puts out? What happens when the values and principles of the organisation are ignored or bypassed for expediency?

Unfortunately these breaks in consistency across an organisation are all too frequent. These are the type of disconnects that cause the majority of brands to become the 'also-rans' in the market. The strongest brands continue to flourish at the expense of the others — and it has absolutely nothing to do with size.

It has everything to do with perceptions and experiences:

- Perceptions and experience rule, not the product
- They occur every time someone comes into contact with the organisation
- They happen at every level
- They can be positive or negative
- There are internal perceptions and experiences as well as external ones
- Perceptions and experience create a culture
- They can be mismanaged, ignored or controlled
- They can be divisive as well as cohesive
- They should be managed from board level down, across the entire organisation
- They must not be left to chance and external happenstance
- They can be controlled only through consistency in all situations

Therefore, identifying these disconnects is of paramount importance if you want to build a strong brand, because they all affect experiences and perceptions. The advantages are obvious. The organisation will begin to gain dominance within the market, products can begin to be promoted at a premium because of the brand reputation, and the marketing budget will show a marked improvement on ROI. Recruitment will be easier, and there will be lower levels of absenteeism, better performance and greater profitability. In times of turndown or recession, the brand will be in a much stronger position to maintain market share. Such an organisation will attract better exit terms for proprietors, gain greater strength in mergers or takeover situations, and generally have a much healthier existence. Yes it takes time and hard work, but the rewards are there for those who persevere.

The important factor here is to understand that discovering where the disconnects lie is never negative. True, the disconnect itself can have a negative influence, but understanding where and what the disconnects are, can only ever bring positive results! Fixing disconnects always strengthens the brand.

So how do you discover where these disconnects are? Some will be obvious from the answers you gave to the diagnostic statements. Some will need some soul searching and some will require simple team work. Going back to the brand wheel, we said the area of character was the foundation on which to build the wall. **Statement 1** comes from this area: 'we have a clear sense of mission that is shared by everyone in the organisation'. Look at where your agreement level lies between 'strongly agree' and 'strongly disagree'. Let us assume you were 'inclined to agree'.

Now look at **statement 6**: 'staff at all levels are excited about the direction the organisation is taking'. How did you score on **statement 6**? Was it the same as for **statement 1**? If you 'were inclined to disagree', then you have a disconnect!

The key we gave you for **statement 1** was 'is it shared by everyone?' If you believed that was largely true, then the key to **statement 6** which was 'how do you know?' should accurately reinforce your answer to **statement 1**. If you couldn't easily quantify **statement 6**, then you have to question the validity of a positive answer to **statement 1**, because without validation, then the first answer is nothing more than an assumption.

The principle here is that if you stated that your sense of mission is 'shared by everyone', then you must ensure that all staff become excited about the direction. You should be able to validate your discovering where the **disconnects** lie is never negative

answers but, if not, then work needs to be done to rectify this. This is at the heart of culture, changing negative to positive, changing reactive to proactive, and validating those changes through constant communication.

There is another type of disconnect that can occur here as well. If your answer to **statement 1** was rather negative, and the answer to **statement 6** was also rather negative, there is even more work that needs doing! This will mean crafting a holistic brand strategy (see chapter 3), imparting the vision, and then setting about creating a culture in line with the brand manifesto.

Here is another possible set of disconnects. Check out your answer to **statement 7** – if you have a structured process in place for rewarding exceptional performance, together with staff appraisals and salary review processes, then your answer is probably a fairly positive agreement. How did you score on **statement 11**? Very low staff turnover? Great! However, a more negative answer could either indicate that the staff do not appreciate the rewards, or more probably that your answer to **statement 10** was not entirely positive. Recruiting staff according to your brand strategy will mean that you are careful in selecting people who 'fit' the brand. The fact they can meet the job specification should be a given before the interview process begins. Once this has been tested, then 'fit' becomes the dominant point of choice. Negative personalities can be difficult to integrate into a positive culture. On the other hand, potential employees that demonstrate the same values as the brand will live the brand on a daily basis.

There is always a crossover point in beginning to build a holistic brand strategy where employees are embedded into the company that were not recruited according to a brand profile. You will have to live with this situation and work with such people to take on board the new brand culture and live and work by brand principles. Some will become brand champions, and some will be a proverbial pain in the...! There is only so much you can do, and a parting of the ways is sometimes more beneficial for both the employee and the business. The process always depends on getting buy-in from everyone (see chapter 4) and takes time, effort and great teamwork.

We have looked briefly for possible causes of disconnection between the areas of character and personality. The next disconnects can occur between the area of talents and voice.

How did you answer **statement 12**? The key was do you regularly review? Let us assume that you don't, so your answer would be 'strongly disagree'. So how did you answer **statement 17**? If you feel that the pricing structure is driven by reputation, then you might have answered 'inclined to agree'. Now check **statement 18**. How did you answer this one? Do you really know you deliver value-for-money, or did you assume? Finally check **statement 14**. Again you should regularly review the factors that influence your customers buying decisions. If you don't then your answer should be in the area of 'disagree'. You can see how disconnects can occur, just through generalised assumptions without strategically conducted analysis.

Another disconnect can occur between **statements 15** and **16**. Another can occur for **statements 9** and **20**. Another could be between **statements 4** and **13**. Look at your answers and check if you are consistent, or whether you may have some disconnects.

Don't worry! Most companies have all sorts of disconnects going on. Understanding yours while they persist in theirs just gains you a competitive advantage!

Other disconnects can occur within any of the four areas of the brand wheel, and across any of the four areas from one to another. As we said at the beginning of this chapter, all companies have different shaped stones in their brand wall, and so it would be impossible to give you an accurate diagnosis of where your particular disconnects occur. You can see from these few examples of how divisive and potentially dangerous these disconnects can be to the organisation if not tackled at the root of the problem. Left unchecked they will spread to cause untold damage to a brand, stifle growth potential, and limit employee performance, among other things. Carry your disconnects forward with you as you begin to implement your brand, and deal with them in a structured manner.

Chapter 9

Summing it all up

Holistic branding is a lifetime activity. What we have tried to do with this book has been to encourage you to reshape your thought processes and to take a step back from the traditional viewpoint of brand. Brand as identity alone is no longer sufficient for the business of the 21st century. Brand as a marketing tool alone falls a long way short of the real value to be won from a well constructed and consistently delivered strategy. The real winners in today's business climate are the forward thinking companies who take that holistic view and use it to create a delivery culture that supports and enhances marketing activity.

Brand, when articulated in terms of its real constituent parts − **character, personality, talents** and **voice** − becomes a powerful tool for change within organisations of any size. Don't be afraid to 'dig deep' to find the rich seam of brand **character** that lies beneath every business. Understanding and living the real values of the organisation, its core purpose and principles means creating a set of behaviours that deliver on the brand promise day in, day out. Setting ambitious, long-term, stretching goals brings a sense of direction that moves the business ever onwards with the whole team pulling together to achieve those goals. This is the beginning of culture − and the consistent delivery of positive experience is only achievable from within a delivery culture.

Building clarity around the brand **personality** allows you to shape the environment in which you operate so that your people can easily live out the culture you have created. To have a consistent internal answer to the question 'what are we like?' means that you can be assured that when your stakeholders consider the same question, they will answer in the same way that you do. This is the beginning of perception management — the cornerstone of understanding and responding to the needs of your customers and your staff. Businesses with 'split' personalities won't fool the world for very long, any more than businesses that continually wear a mask to hide what they are really like.

Getting to grips with your brand **talents** will enable you to create a family of products and services that position you for success. With a product set that is really in tune with your target market, that is priced in line with the value it brings, and that is positioned creatively, you will find differentiation and competition less problematic. The importance of well thought through product management is paramount. Without it, the best strategies in the world will fail because the product doesn't hold up to expectations. The key to managing brand talents is rigourous and regular review. Its not enough to rely on what worked in the market ten years, five years or even one year ago. Research, research, research!

Finally, it's time to define and build your brand **voice**. You will find that in the context of the rest of your brand understanding, building messages and allowing creative freedom delivers real dividends. It is possible to turn on its head the old adage '50% of advertising works, but who knows which 50%'. Not only is it possible, in today's lean marketplace, it's essential. Return on investment for creativity, innovation and design is essential for successful business. To approach design and marketing from a wholly tactical standpoint is to forego the value of the strategic context of holistic branding that brings long-term value.

With an articulated brand, a managed culture and a sense of excitement about the future, now is the time to build the brand strategy – **brand manifesto**, **brand plan** and **brand delivery**. Building the defined culture in to a **brand manifesto** will enable the business to create a framework for the creation of functional activities such as recruitment policy, staff development and customer service. The **brand manifesto** is the key element of strategy in that it forms the foundation of the delivery culture. This is so essential when building a company that is dedicated to quality, service and customer relationship management. The **brand manifesto** also contains the description of the landscape in which the company operates, both in terms of marketplace and business environment. These are key elements that ground the manifesto in the reality of the working environment and ensure that the delivery of excellence is focused on a desire to serve the customer and position the business for success.

Building a **brand plan** will allow real-time assessment of progress towards goals. To reiterate the words of Churchill, *'however beautiful the strategy, you should occasionally look at the results'.* No strategy is worth the paper it's written on if it doesn't have relevant planning built in so that the individual elements of the strategy can be managed, measured and assessed. Incorporating capacity planning, resource management and risk mitigation, a good plan is essential to the delivery of a solid brand experience. Marketing strategy can also be included in the brand plan to ensure that marketing activity is undertaken in line with internal brand delivery. The **brand plan** is the architect's drawing that allows the building of the brand from the ground up.

The last area of the brand strategy is to define the **brand delivery**. This is the part of the strategy where the organisation can design and record the processes required to 'do it now, do it well and do it again'.

Talking about delivery is not enough. To build real value in the brand requires that the business build mechanisms for delivery that are immediate, quality focused and replicable. In the end, your customers return because they have an experience of your business that is sufficiently attractive to sway their buying decisions in your favour – time and again. There is a constant imperative for the holistically branded organisation to identify, document, deliver, measure and review processes that ensure the delivery of a consistently high standard of experience.

So now it's over to you. We've taken your crayons from you and we've given them back! It's up to you now whether you use them in context to give you the best opportunity of building a strong holistic brand. It will be a challenge and it will take an investment of time, commitment and energy, but the results will be dramatic. Embrace the concept of the holistic brand and you will be on the road to building a company that is focused, envisioned and consistently delivering. You will begin to see the effect on your bottom line as profitability increases and customer retention improves – and you will add significant value to your business. You can do it, your people can do it, your customers want it and your stakeholders demand it – **so go ahead and build your brand!**

Diagnostic scorecard

Diagnostic scorecard

Score key

1	Strongly disagree
2	Inclined to disagree
3	Neither agree nor disagree
4	Inclined to agree
5	Strongly agree

1	We have a clear sense of mission that is shared by everyone in the organisation	score
2	The organisation is quick to learn from both successes and failures	score
3	We regularly review our reputation with our customers, our suppliers and our staff	score
4	Our staff can articulate the differences between our organisation and our competitors	score
5	This organisation never compromises its core principles	score
6	Personnel at all levels are excited about the direction the organisation is taking	score

7	Exceptional performance is always recognised and rewarded	score
8	Working practices in the organisation have changed as a result of market trends	score
9	Our market share has increased in the last twelve months	score
10	Our recuitment policy has been developed as a result of work undertaken on our vision and values	score
11	We have a very low staff turnover rate	score
12	We regularly review our product placement strategy	score
13	Our product support differs significantly from that of our competitors	score
14	We regularly review the factors that influence our customers' buying decisions	score
15	We are happy with our current customer retention levels	score
16	Our customer service is as good as it can be	score
17	Our pricing strategy is driven more by our reputation than by other factors	score
18	Our customers believe that we deliver value-for-money	score
19	Our profit margins are increasing	score
20	We can quantify return on investment for our marketing spend	score

Your total score

Appendix 2
Diagnostic evaluation

Score range   Overall rating

85-100

Highly effective

Your brand works well across the organisation. Operational activities are strongly aligned with your brand values. Your marketing is effective, you have a good reputation among your stakeholders and your organisation is growing.

Care should be taken to ensure that you have strategies in place to build on your current strengths.

70-84

Generally effective

Your brand is generally working well and there are many positive areas of your business. There are areas of your business that are not aligned well with your brand values and, as a result, your growth and performance does not match the organisation's full potential.

Work to identify misalignments in the organisation, and to build a cohesive strategy to implement brand values across the board should be considered.

50-69

Somewhat effective

Whilst there are areas of your brand that are working well, the positive impact of this is lessened by a lack of cohesion across the organisation in terms of the application of vision and values across functional areas.

In order to flourish in your marketplace, you should begin to identify your brand and to build a long-term strategy for your brand that you can roll out across the organisation. The benefits of this will be realised very quickly, both internally and externally.

Score range	Overall rating

30-49

Somewhat ineffective

Whilst there are some areas of your organisation that are performing well, the effect of your brand is low in terms of differentiating you from your competition. As a result, growth is disappointing and you are not getting the value that you could from your brand. There are considerable areas of misalignment and your customer experience is inconsistent.

You need help to move the business to the next level in terms of growth and profitability. By focusing internally on how you can apply vision and values to the way that your organisation works, you will begin to reap the rewards of better customer retention and increased profitability.

less than 30

Generally ineffective

You already know that there are serious issues in your organisation that hinder growth and have a negative impact on your profitability.

You should urgently seek help to start to build your brand and a long-term strategy to implement your brand both externally and internally. Organisational change is essential to growth.

A to Z of holistic branding benefits

This list is not exhaustive. Feel free to add your own as you discover them. As an organisation becomes more holistically attuned, the more the benefits are revealed. Whether you concentrate on a local area marketplace, trade on a national scale or even participate by trading in the global arena, these benefits are true for all companies that align all their experiences and perceptions into one recognisable brand.

In this situation, prices can be placed at a premium, and long-term contracts (both individual and corporate) can more easily be obtained because the offering is seen to be consistent and dependable. This adds real value in exit negotiations.

A to Z of holistic branding benefits

Aligns all channels of communication

Brand awareness rises

Customer experiences and perceptions become positive

Direction becomes clear to all stakeholders

Equity in the brand becomes a valuable asset

Future planning will benefit from a predetermined brand strategy

Gravitas can be established in the market

Holistic approach eliminates mixed media messages

Integrity is better assured

Joint benefits created for customers and the organisation

Keeps every aspect of the business working together

Lower recruitment costs because staff churn is reduced

Morale improves because the culture improves

Negative comments controlled and minimised

Overheads reduce through aligned processes

Profitability improves

Quantifies the business

Recruitment opportunities increase

Sales opportunities improve through differentiation

Trust in the brand is maximised

Underpins company behaviour, principles and values

Value-for-money proposition overrides price

Works for all types of businesses, across all sectors

X-factor created by holistic branding provides USPs

Your 'vision' actually means something!

Zoological classification of customers is rationalised